Also by
BRUCE JAY FRIEDMAN

NONFICTION
The Lonely Guy's Book of Life

NOVELS
Stern
A Mother's Kisses
The Dick
About Harry Towns
Tokyo Woes
The Current Climate

SHORT STORY COLLECTIONS
Far From the City of Class
Black Angels
Let's Hear It for a Beautiful Guy

PLAYS
Steambath
Scuba Duba

The
Slightly
Older Guy

BRUCE JAY FRIEDMAN

SIMON & SCHUSTER

NEW YORK   LONDON   TORONTO

SYDNEY   TOKYO   SINGAPORE

SIMON & SCHUSTER
Rockefeller Center
1230 Avenue of the Americas
New York, NY 10020

SIMON & SCHUSTER and colophon are registered trademarks
of Simon & Schuster Inc.

Designed by Elina D. Nudelman

Manufactured in the United States of America

10 9 8 7 6 5 4 3 2 1

Library of Congress Cataloging-in-Publication Data
Friedman, Bruce Jay, date.
   The slightly older guy / Bruce J. Friedman.
       p.   cm.
   1. Middle aged men—Humor.   2. Man-woman
relationships—Humor.   I. Title.
PS3556.R5S58   1995
818'.5402—dc20   95-9759
                                        CIP

ISBN 0-684-80206-6

For Molly and Max—
Slightly Older Guys of the Future

CONTENTS

Introduction: Who (or What) Is a Slightly Older Guy? / 11

Part One / Exploring the New Territory

Telltale Signs That You're a Member of the Club, *17*
Chin Fat, *20*
Speak, Memory—Please, *22*
Sex and the Slightly Older Guy, *26*
Insults and Rejections, *31*

Part Two / Shaping Up

A Diet for the Slightly Older Guy, *39*
Earrings and Ponytails, *45*
A Wardrobe Update, *50*
At the Baseline, *52*
Some Other Roads to Fitness, *57*
"The Doctor Will See You Now," *60*
Two Sinful Pursuits, *65*

Part Three / Affairs of the Heart

A Circle of Friends, *71*
Divorce—and the Ex-Wife, *77*
The Slightly Older Wife, *79*
The Slightly Older Guy and His Kids, *83*
Dating—and the Eleventh-Hour Romance, *87*
A Young Wife, *93*

Part Four / Affairs of the Pocketbook

Some Small and Painless Economies, *101*
The (Forcibly) Retired Slightly Older Guy (and Some
    Career Opportunities), *106*
The Last Word: Wills, Burial Plots, Epitaphs, *113*

Part Five / The Large Arena

A Run for Office, *121*
A Word About P.C., *126*

Part Six / Ease On Down the Road

Making Your Life Comfortable, *131*
Back on the Highway, *135*
Slightly Older Guy Treats, *140*
The Country Life, *146*

Part Seven / The Future—Such as It Is

Get Ready to Meet Your Maker, *153*
In Sum, *156*

Introduction
Who (or What) Is a Slightly Older Guy?

It takes him a little longer than it once did to get out of restaurant booths. But once he's on his feet, he stretches out a bit and breaks into the easy casual stride of a professional athlete, which he may never have been. He thinks about bran a lot. Is he getting enough bran? It seems that everywhere he goes he hears the word "pops" and assumes it's directed at him.

The Slightly Older Guy goes to pieces if someone criticizes his work, and he's become insecure about his appeal to women, even if (in the past) they've fallen at his feet. He worries about Trollope a lot. Shouldn't he be reading Trollope before it's too late? He's concerned that he may never see Kuala Lumpur, even though it has Burger Kings. He's tempted to write his memoirs, but is embarrassed because he's never slept with anyone famous. He hesitates before taking out a long-term auto lease for fear of being survived by a Mazda. And he wishes the medical establishment would make up its mind about the prostate. (Do something about it or leave it alone.)

If you wake up one morning with the sinking feeling that you're a Slightly Older Guy, don't panic. Not just yet. For one thing, you're in good company. Chevy Chase is a Slightly Older Guy and Bill Clinton is becoming one as we speak. Former Secretary of the Treasury Lloyd Bentsen may be out of the loop, but you have Rod Stewart for company, especially when he's singing and dancing with young rock-

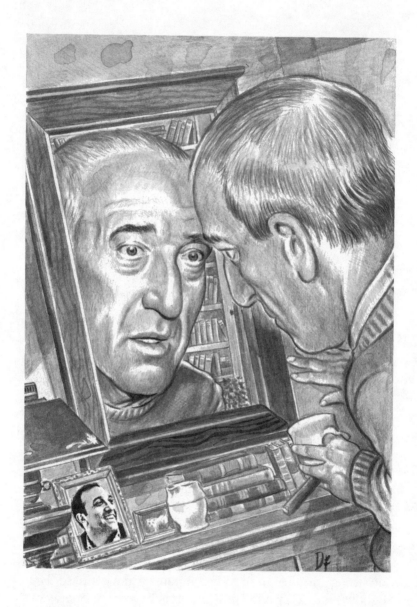

ers and is a little bit behind the beat. Dustin Hoffman has Slightly Older Guy written all over him, with all the attendant ramifications for his career. Howard Stern makes the list because of his serious concerns about his sexual organ, as does Robin Williams, if only he would sit still for a minute.

CNN is loaded with Slightly Older Guys, and NBC's Tom Brokaw, despite being winsome, has been one for some time. Warren Beatty, George Plimpton, Yasir Arafat, Candice Bergen (oops)—but why go on?

It would be nice to report that there are rich golden opportunities ahead for the Slightly Older Guy, but quite honestly very few come to mind. There's folk dancing, of course. If you're a folk dancer, you should be positioned nicely. But if you're part of the vast majority of Slightly Older Guys who don't folk dance, the territory you're about to enter is bleak and uncharted. Mistakes cannot be made. One stumble here and it's time for the fat lady.

What follows are some thoughts on how to survive this rough patch so that you're in decent condition when you break out into the clear and become a Considerably Older Guy—at which time you'll be sought out for your advice on the deficit and asked if we should go to war.

BJF
Water Mill, New York
(Division Headquarters for the Slightly Older Guy)

Part One

Exploring the New Territory

Telltale Signs That You're a Member of the Club

"It's true I'm getting on a bit," you might concede begrudgingly, "but hold on a second. I'm feeling fine and I didn't have a care in the world until this subject came up. Before I start worrying, how do I know for sure I'm a Slightly Older Guy?"

To begin with, there's no point in worrying about it. Once you've crossed the line, there's no turning back, and worrying will only make it worse. But in case you need proof, here are some signs that you've become an official member of the club.

- *You're sitting at a bar* that's filled with attractive young people on their way home from work. You catch the reflection in the mirror of a fellow who is clearly out of place and wonder, with some irritation, why he doesn't push on to a watering hole that's more appropriate to his obviously advancing years. In horror you realize, hey, wait a minute, that's me!

- *You notice subtle changes in your body*—a slight sharpening of the elbows, an unwelcome latticework about the eyes, an odd new configuration of the knees. You can't quite put your finger on it—they're not

17

exactly knobby—but they're not the knees
you once knew and loved. Come to think of it,
they don't perform as effectively as they once
did—and your physician has made a subtle
mention of arthroscopic repair, quickly
reassuring you that nose tackles have it done
virtually every week.

- *You've had sex*—a week or so ago—and it's
probably time for another go-round. It
crosses your mind that maybe you ought to
hold off for a bit—and ration it out, so to
speak.

- *You run into a contemporary* you haven't
seen in years and you're shocked by how
much the poor fellow has aged.

- *On a bus,* you focus in on an attractive young
woman and entertain thoughts about asking
her out for a drink. She looks up, smiles, and
says sweetly, "Would you care to have my
seat?"

- *Your college alumni bulletin rolls in* and you
note with discomfort that your class notes are
sliding closer to the head of the list—a
position you'd always assumed was reserved
for a handful of hardy ninety-year-olds who
were on hand when the college was first
endowed.

- *It occurs to you that* you've been attending
quite a few funerals recently—and that
conversational topics like "quadruple
bypasses," "organ transplants," and "hip

replacements" are right up there with sports scores and the stock market.

- *You're forced to take aside a certain friend* who's only a few years ahead of you and ask him if he'd mind not prefacing his remarks with the phrase "Now that we're in the twilight years."

- *You find yourself sucking in your stomach* in public and notice that none of your pants fit comfortably. Rather than let them out, you loosen the belt a notch or two, keep the waist unfastened, and decide to change dry cleaners. Obviously, the one you have is shrinking your suits.

- *You make it through the night* without a trip to the bathroom and consider it a cause for celebration.

If all of this sounds familiar, don't worry, there's no need to lose it and start folding your tent. Once you've gotten yourself to admit manfully that you are, indeed, a Slightly Older Guy, the trick is to see this new phase of life as an adventure, with surprises popping up at every turn. Some, of course, will be unwelcome. But there are strategies for dealing with them, many of which will be set forth in the pages that follow—assuming that the author can still remember them.

Chin Fat

One of the first things you're going to have to deal with as a Slightly Older Guy is chin fat,* which generally rolls in overnight. You go to bed thinking, "I'll bet I'm one of the lucky ones who will never get chin fat," and the next morning there it is.

No one is immune. Not Paul Newman. Not even Robert Redford. Kevin Johnson of the Phoenix Suns will eventually develop some, and Clint Eastwood already has a fold of it, although his comes across as being sinewy and windswept. The critic Harold Bloom has literary chin fat; he may be hiding a small poet in there. The only people who don't have to worry about it are the Rev. Al Sharpton and pleasant moon-faced types who have had it their whole lives.

There is no need to drag Dan Rather into this.

Your first impulse when chin fat appears is to pat and slap it with the back of the hand in an attempt to press it down; then, with increasing frustration, to grab and yank at it. None of this is useful and may even serve to stretch it out a bit. (Happily, there are no recorded cases of people who've died from an overload of chin fat.)

The Good Fight

Chin fat is going to be with you from here on in, so you may as well get used to it. Here are some civilized ways for the Slightly Older Guy to cope with this unpleasant reality:

---

* A.k.a. rope neck, wattles.

- Instruct children that they are not to hop on your lap and tug at it—or, in the case of hyperactive youngsters, to take hold of it and attempt to swing back and forth.

- Advise young wives and girlfriends that it is not helpful to say, "Oh, I don't know. I think it's kinda cute."

- In public places, learn to whip your head around dramatically at intervals as if you've heard a gunshot. This will, for brief periods, flatten out your accumulation.

- Spend a great deal of time reclining on couches, with your head thrown back, staring languidly into space. This, too, will pull back your folds dramatically for as long as you can hold the position. (For guidance, refer to Truman Capote's early book jacket photos.)

- Grow a beard.

- The face-lift, of course, is an option, although there will always be someone around to whisper: "Don't you think he's done a remarkable job with his chin fat?" (Suddenly showing up in turtlenecks will not fool the observant.)

Finally, the philosophical stance is the only feasible one. There is no need to jiggle your chin fat about flamboyantly in the manner of the late film actor S. Z. "Cuddles" Sakall, but you might as well accept it. After all, isn't it just more of *you* to love?

Go with your chin fat.

Speak, Memory—Please

At some point, as a Slightly Older Guy, you're going to find yourself standing in the kitchen in your bathrobe, wondering *what on earth you're doing there.* Your first response might be to pound on the wall and cry, "For God's sake, why am I here?" Or, with moderation, to tap your temple encouragingly and prod, "Come on, pal. You can remember why you're in the kitchen. Give it a try."

Memory loss is an unsettling experience, but you're probably just overreacting. What you want to do is calmly take hold of yourself, put the whole business out of your mind, and as long as you're in the kitchen, make some productive use of the time. Dice up a cucumber, for example, or get rid of some old croissants. Once you've engaged in some such purposeful activity, it's likely that in no time at all you'll recall that you came into the kitchen for a liverwurst sandwich. It's possible you've forgotten to buy liverwurst, but that's a different issue.

Discouraging as such an experience may be, there's probably a simple explanation for it. You may have been preoccupied with some larger concern, such as whether we ought to take a stiffer position with the Japanese on barley imports or to throw our weight behind Crimea in its efforts to break away from Ukraine. Perhaps you'd been leafing through the *New England Journal of Medicine,* dipped into another one of their cholesterol diatribes, and decided to cut back on your liverwurst consumption. Or maybe you've just about had it with liverwurst.

Unfortunately, such explanations will be of little consolation to the Slightly Older Guy, who'll tend to be extremely sensitive about his memory. Cast the slightest doubt on his ability to recall and he'll snappishly rattle off a list of the Scottish kings. What he's forgotten is that his memory has always had a few gaps. How many times have you forgotten to pick up a gallon of milk on the way home? Or to come home at all, for that matter?

Was there ever a time when you could distinguish between Chita Rivera and Rita Moreno?

So You've Slipped a Little . . .

Let's allow for a moment that your memory isn't quite what it once was. How much of it do you require? It's one thing to forget a favorite shashlik recipe, but do you really need to remember the exact content of sixteenth-century papal bulls? Isn't it enough to recall their drift? Or perhaps to focus on the ones that annoyed Martin Luther? How often will you be called on to describe the battlefield at Tannenberg? Or to hold forth on Mameluke tactics at Ain Jalut? It's one thing to have a fund of anecdotes about Lenin's fear of hair loss, but what if you forget a few? Do you really think your friends will think less of you? Find some other way to amuse them. Buy them a drink for a change.

And let's say the entire siege of Malta suddenly vanishes from your mind, as if Malta had never undergone a siege. Will it make you less desirable as a dinner guest? It's highly unlikely. What's more probable is that with the obscure factual data gone from your mind, you'll find yourself running a leaner, tighter operation. Like Chrysler.

There's also the new Information Highway. Don't forget about that. With this baby running, all you need to do is slip into your study, boot up your system, and march out triumphantly with a full accounting of Turkey's naval strategy at Lepanto. That is, should your expertise be called into question.

Some Opportunities

If your memory has gone off by a hair, is there any reason why you can't use this alleged deficiency to your advantage? Let's say you've become confused about your accountant's number and somehow got Julia Roberts on the phone. Isn't it a perfect opportunity to strike up a conversation? Ask her about the competing demands of career and marriage—and whether she and Lyle have been able to adjust to the Hollywood community. There's no telling where such a conversation may lead.

Or what if you've set out on a trip to Atlanta and somehow ended up in Fayetteville? Instead of doubling back in frustration, why not stay right where you are and use the occasion to find out what makes the place tick? Just what is it that makes Fayetteville Fayetteville?

Thanks for Your Memory

For the Slightly Older Guy who continues to be upset about his forgetfulness, it's much more advantageous to think of your memory—although not quite as robust as it once was—as the good friend that it's always been, enabling you to forget dentist appointments and to remember forty dollars you stashed in an old windbreaker; to blot out entire failed marriages, yet retain in exquisite detail a night spent in the arms of a Sausalito folksinger; to forget you were ever described as an "ingrate" in a company newsletter and to remember instead the farewell dinner in your honor, one in which toasts were proposed to your sales record and you were sent off with a pair of monogrammed pajamas. In short, focus on a memory that's canceled out your defeats, highlighted your triumphs, and led you to think of your life for the most part as a series of happy events.

Above all, be grateful to the memory that enables you to forget now and then that you've joined the ranks of America's Slightly Older Guys.

Sex and the Slightly Older Guy

As a Slightly Older Guy, there's no need to say goodbye to your sex life, although it's true that you may have to make a few adjustments here and there. To put it in baseball terms, it's no longer realistic to rely on your high, hard one.

To survive in the romantic league, you've got to develop a slider.

Help from Your Heroes

As a younger fellow, all that was required of you was to show up—and the deed was half done. If you show up now —and that's all you do, show up—you may be asked to leave the premises. As a Slightly Older Guy, you'll have to call on all of your wisdom and experience to keep you in the game. And don't feel you're necessarily working at a handicap. Think of the great George Blanda, still kicking field goals in his forties; "Ancient Archie" Moore, a terror in the ring at fifty-five; Satchel Paige, racking up strikeouts at God knows what age. Don't think of these legendary figures while you're *having* sex—and certainly don't cry out their names for inspiration—but at quiet moments give some thought to them as role models.

The Old Pro

As a first step in moving to the next tier of your sex life, try to rid yourself of Performance Anxiety. The very word *performance* is misleading. It isn't as if you have to trot out on stage and play the ukelele. It's not like that, of course, although once you're in front of the footlights you will have to do more than just stare at the audience. Remember that you have considerable experience in this area—probably more than you recollect—and it isn't just a matter of having once mastered erotic toe manipulation in the Philippines. For example, there are no doubt a wealth of erogenous zones you can call to mind if you take a minute to think about them. Write them down and you'll be amazed at the length of the list before you even get to the inner thigh. And each of your lovers has probably passed along a trick or two which you can call into play with your current part- ner—although there's no need to credit your source when you do. When your bed partner sighs and says, "That was wonderful," don't tell her you learned it from a saleswoman at Neiman Marcus.

If you can summon the energy, you'll find that even as a Slightly Older Guy you're a whole bundle of sexuality.

Here are a few fundamentals you might want to give some thought to before you get under way.

LIGHTS, MUSIC!

Generally speaking, lights should be warm and nonthreat- ening. Harsh fluorescents will put your partner in mind of a gynecological checkup. Admittedly, this can be arousing now and then, but to be on the safe side, keep the lights low. (Besides, as a Slightly Older Guy, you don't want your lover getting too good a look at your waistline.)

EYES LIKE DEEP POOLS

The most formidable of defenses will crumble under a hail of flattery. Keep your complimentary remarks personal. Direct them to hair, perhaps, or fragrance, but not necessarily to decorating skills. And you don't want to make too much of your partner's love-making experience or draw undue attention to specific body parts.

As a rule of thumb, and provided compliments are framed tastefully, you can't fire off enough of them.

VARIETY

It may be that your presentation has become predictable and it's time to approach your lover from a different direction. If so, it will add more spice to the experience if you don't announce your plans in advance. Capitalize on the element of surprise.

And vary the locale now and then, although as a Slightly Older Guy it is wise to select a soft surface, wherever it might be.

You might try sex with your clothes on now and then. Or even switching clothes as long as there's general agreement beforehand that all items are to be returned to their original owner.

FANTASIZE

A standard method of adding savor to your lovemaking is to imagine that your partner is someone else—Sharon Stone, Bridget Fonda, Margaret Thatcher, anyone you're not in bed with at the time. Or imagine *you* are someone else—Judge Ito if you really want to get wild. No one's checking up on you. (A line should be drawn at Helmut Kohl.)

For a truly great stimulant, you might want to try a little-used formula which involves thinking of *the person you're actually making love to*. But don't overwork this approach. It is only effective if it's used sparingly.

BE YOURSELF

The best way to behave in bed is the way you behave out of it, which is what got you into bed in the first place. Don't assume an entirely different personality just because you happen to be naked. You may be a Slightly Older Guy, but *you're* the one who's been chosen as a lover, not Danny DeVito.

Positions: Scaling Back

The Slightly Older Guy who's accustomed to working with thirty or forty positions should think in terms of reducing that number to half a dozen or so. Eliminate those that involve a great deal of thrashing about and call for strenuous hip and leg movements. Also ones that require the use of some overhead appurtenance to keep your balance. Ideally, you want to keep the positions that offer maximum comfort and support so you won't do any permanent damage to your lower back.

A Salute to the Big Fella

A word here about your equipment, or the Big Fella, as you may have generously dubbed him after a successful romp in Tijuana many moons ago. It isn't as if he's been off on his own all these years. He's been with you through every campaign, a close and valued member of the team who's stuck by you through thick and thin, which is more than you can say for some of your friends. He may have faltered here and there, but he's never given less than his all in your behalf. And on those few occasions when he's gone on furlough, he's soon returned cheerfully to the fray. He was there with you at your first dance, every bit as tremulous and uncertain as you were, and stayed on even though there were times when he arrived at the front, ready to do his duty, only to discover that his services were not required, forcing him to retire to the barracks in frustration.

He's shared the strenuous and rollicking days of your youth, when he was asked to go forward blindly into unfamiliar and bizarre situations. He's with you now, at a presumably more peaceful time, just as loyal as ever but perhaps a bit weary now that you've become a Slightly Older Guy. Hasn't he become a Slightly Older Guy, too? Just be patient and don't expect more from him than you yourself can deliver. Treat the old boy with kindness and respect. When the bugle calls, you may be surprised to find that he will rally round and march proudly at your side, once again bringing honor to your banner—the banner of a Slightly Older Guy who's still very much in the parade.

Insults and Rejections

As a Slightly Older Guy, you'll find that your feel-ings are much closer to the surface than ever before. An unreturned phone call, the failure of a headwaiter to greet you with ceremony, a young woman addressing you as "Sir" —any one of these occurrences will be enough to plunge you into despair. You may start thinking someone's out to get you. But you've merely become a victim of heightened sensitivity. Let's not forget. You're a Slightly Older Guy. It goes with the territory.

Here are some touchy areas—and some strategies on how to cope with them.

"Why Him and Not Me?"

The success of a friend or contemporary, once a minor nuisance, will now come across as a personal affront. Be careful that your response isn't disproportionate. Don't start resenting an engineer friend's appointment to adviser of the shuttle program and forget that your own background is in dinette fixtures. Or become annoyed at Joe Pesci for being chosen over you as Best Supporting Actor at the Academy Awards when you've never been in front of a camera and Pesci has been slaving away at his craft for years.

Pesci may have gotten wind of some of *your* achievements. Maybe he's heard that you were named entertainment director of your condo and he's upset about *that*.

More important is that Pesci wasn't given the Oscar just to make you feel awful. The members of the academy have probably never heard of you. (And don't let that set you off.)

The main thing is to forget Pesci and get some kind of life.

Don't Push It

When it comes to women, the Slightly Older Guy may find himself becoming particularly thin-skinned. If a woman flirts with him, it won't for a second occur to him that she finds him attractive. His first impulse will be to get out of town before she comes to her senses. Or, at the other extreme, he'll start to behave too aggressively, marching up with unnatural boldness to beautiful women. And when, for example, supermodel Elle McPherson politely declines his invitation to go to Barbados for the weekend, he is absolutely certain she's turning him down because he's a Slightly Older Guy.

Here again, a little detachment is in order. For one thing, Elle McPherson might not care for Barbados. Maybe it's just not her scene. Or it may be that she's been there on so many shoots that Barbados is coming out of her ears. Or perhaps she's got something going with Brad Pitt and wants to see how it plays out before she makes any new commitments.

"That's all very nice," you might say to yourself, "but if I was a young guy, I'll bet she would've hopped right on that plane."

Not necessarily. Even if that were the case, she might have wanted to find out just a little bit more about you. Give McPherson some room and she might surprise you by coming round. And if for some reason she doesn't, you can always try Claudia Schiffer.

The Restaurant Challenge

The restaurant is an arena that's sure to test the Slightly Older Guy's ego. Touchy to an extreme, he'll stride into a four-star restaurant and demand to be seated at Woody Allen's table, even if the legendary little filmmaker is right there in the middle of his dinner.

If you've been behaving in this manner, you're definitely out of line. What you've got to realize is that even though you've seen all of Allen's pictures and have been supporting the man for years, he may not *want* you at his table on this particular evening. Maybe he's entertaining some friends from out of town. Or trying to get Daniel Day-Lewis to work for scale in his next picture. You can't expect him to make room for you because he doesn't want to hurt your feelings. Take the high ground and accept a table next to Allen's where you can wave to him now and then and occasionally lean over and offer some opinions about cinematographers.

"I'll Get Back to You"

The failure of a friend or colleague to return a call immediately is a fact of life—but not to the Slightly Older Guy who'll no doubt see it as further evidence that the cards are stacked against him. Yet there are any number of reasons why your call hasn't been returned. Maybe your friend has had an attack of laryngitis. Or he's busy fending off a sexual harassment suit. If he's an agent, it's possible he's left for another agency.

Don't sit around and brood about any of this. Make an omelette while you're waiting. Sandpaper something or start reading *Middlemarch.* If he hasn't returned your call in twenty minutes, arrange to be unavailable when he does finally get back to you.

Where's My Invitation?

Inevitably, you'll hear of a party to which you haven't been invited.

"That's it for me socially," you'll conclude sadly. "No one wants a Slightly Older Guy hanging around and dampening the festivities."

There are any number of reasons why you might not have gotten an invitation. Here are just a few:

- *Someone you hate* is going to be there, and the host, out of respect for your feelings, has removed you from the guest list.

- *You're being saved* for a more important party, in honor of Morley Safer.

- *You did get an invitation* but the doorman intercepted it. He's over there now, living it up.

- *The host knew of several other competing parties* and took it for granted you were unavailable—not realizing you weren't invited to those parties either.

Just don't sulk and carry on about this. Plenty of other parties will come along. Sooner or later everyone is invited to *something*.

On-the-Job Sensitivity

It's conceivable you'll survive rebuffs from fashion models and headwaiters, but the inevitably sly comments about your work are going to sting. Suddenly you'll be told that your drawings aren't "hip" enough, or maybe that your last

presentation to the dairy farmers lacked a certain contemporary edge. Try to stand firm. There's a strong chance it's just part of a campaign to get you to lower your price. If they're in a jam and no one else is available, you'll be told your work has taken on a new freshness and vitality.

The Ten Best . . .

Sooner or later, a list is going to be published that you're not on. A list of achievers, people who live in the Hamptons, people who were at some terrific party while you were at home, brooding. Slightly Older Guys are particularly vulnerable to not being included on lists. The way to deal with this is to make it known that you're not interested in lists and that, frankly, you have some questions about the people who make them up. You've heard it's possible to *buy* a place on certain lists, so do they really mean anything? Besides, you're on the only list that really matters—the one that's in the hearts and minds of the people you really care about. If you finally get on one of those socially significant lists, say you're enormously flattered but that you're *still* not interested in them. That's in case you're not on the next one.

Remember that not even George Plimpton makes every list.

Part Two

Shaping Up

A Diet for the Slightly Older Guy

There's no reason to make any drastic changes in your diet. As a Slightly Older Guy, you still need a substantial breakfast to get you off the ground, assuming you're going to get off the ground at all. Generally, it will come down to juice, toast, cereal, pancakes, bacon, and the like in one disappointing combination or another.

If you're frustrated by this tired fare, one way to shake up the dice is to change the order of your meals. This is not to suggest that you kick off the day with couscous and flaming shashlik. But a modest helping of liver and onions in the morning can make for a refreshing change. If you're concerned about the long-term effects of missing an occasional breakfast, you can always polish off a bowl of oatmeal before turning in at night.

The Egg Makes a Comeback

A major innovation in the breakfast arena is in the preparation of eggs. Once feared by the Slightly Older Guy, the egg, when stripped of its yolk, can be consumed in large quantities and is guaranteed to go whistling cleanly through your arteries. Prepared in this manner, eggs even taste a little like eggs. So now might be a good time to revisit this old favorite. Remember, however, that inserting chunks of Polish sausage into an omelette isn't going to help your cause in the least.

Watching Your Weight

Weight control is of particular importance to the Slightly Older Guy. At one time, you may have been able to wave off hip fat, but this is no longer the case. And nobody loves a Slightly Older Guy who's also a Slightly Chubby Guy (a.k.a. a Person of Weight).

Here are some ways to make a dent in those excess pounds.

WATER

Keep water around at all times, and whenever you feel a hunger pang pour out a glassful. You don't have to do this in elevators or on street corners. But keep a pitcher of water in your office and on your night table. Those who've switched to water diets are reported to be thin and clear-eyed, although somewhat fidgety.

HALF A SANDWICH

A novel approach to diet is to prepare any dish you like and *eat only half of it.* Slightly Older Guys have enjoyed great success with this program, their only question being what to do with the other half. Unless you've disposed of it, you're going to find yourself making wistful trips to the kitchen and wondering whether or not to snatch it out of the refrigerator.

One solution is to eat the desired half and feed the remainder to your pet—unless, of course, he's a Slightly Older Dog who is also watching his weight.

Miami restaurants have joined in the spirit of this new movement by serving sandwich halves and withholding the second half, which is reserved in your name and can be picked up the following day. It should be noted that half a Miami sandwich is equal to a whole one in flinty Vermont.

IGNORING THE CLOCK

Another useful dieting measure is to stop being a slave to the clock. Just because it's twelve-thirty, it doesn't mean you have to eat something. There's no one watching you and saying, "It's lunchtime, grab a sandwich or face serious consequences." We're not dealing with a gulag situation here. If you're not hungry, put food out of your mind and do some work for a change. You can eat your meatball hero half an hour later and have all those extra minutes of dieting to your credit.

Foreign Fare

As a Slightly Older Guy, you don't want to spend your precious evenings slaving away over a hot stove. It's important to get out and about and try some of the great new ethnic food that's all over the place.

A few suggestions:

JAPANESE FOOD

Japanese restaurants have become a great favorite and are an excellent way to make social connections. All kinds of fascinating people sit at sushi counters. Your neighbor can turn out to be a Canadian tentmaker—or the owner of another Japanese restaurant. In this relaxed atmosphere, not only will you find yourself making friends, but you'll also be offered all those little pieces of squid that the individual beside you hates.

One of the great attractions of Japanese food is its artistic preparation. It's so beautiful to look at that very often you won't have the heart to eat it, which is in itself slimming. A word of caution, however, about sashimi. Raw fish has been proven to be sexually enhancing and you want to resist the impulse to pinch the waitresses on your way out.

CHINESE FOOD

Chinese food, too, has its allures, although it's not so much the General Tsao's chicken and the thousand-year-old eggs as the conviviality of the staff that makes the dining experience appealing. The warm greeting of a headwaiter ("Welcome back, Mr. Dinsmore. Long time no see") will make you feel you're a turn-of-the-century freebooter in old Shanghai.

STEAKHOUSES

Steakhouses had fallen out of favor, but are miraculously becoming chic again. Most gangland rub-outs take place in such restaurants, which creates a not altogether unpleasant sense of danger in the air. As you dig into your porterhouse and baked potato, there's always the chance that someone in the next booth is going to be slaughtered.

SOME ADVISORIES

Stay away from restaurants that bill themselves as the "Oldest Dining Spot" in town—since they may be serving old food. And the great Nelson Algren's dictum still holds up: "Never eat at a place called 'Mom's,' " with an occasional exception. If *your* mom is the chef, for example.

Don't Forget the Classics

As a Slightly Older Guy, you'll naturally want to see and do it all before the lights get any dimmer. "What's life," you might find yourself asking, "if I've never tasted flamingo haunches or baby goat patties in sweet-and-sour sauce?"

This is understandable, but in reaching out for the exotic, you don't want to turn your back on old favorites that have gotten you to where you are—whether you're pleased about this or not. Take a moment to pay your respects to the banana, for example, which never quite made it as an ice cream flavor but at least is still reliably a banana; to the apple, which is also boring but makes up for it somewhat with its cheerful appearance. Tip your hat to the olive, in all its weirdness, to the cucumber for its stubborn efforts to be interesting, and to lettuce—you know, the old kinds, before the onset of radicchio. Raise your glass to calm, transforming mayonnaise, to the grape, mercifully divested of its seeds, and to the celery stalk, considered worthless by many but proud and magisterial all the same. Pay a tribute to Swiss cheese, relegated to the back of the bus by many, but still royalty to a few diehards; to the unique tomato, if you can find one that tastes like a tomato; and to toast, simple toast, which has seen you through many a queasy stomach —more than you can say for cappellini in lime marinade.

And finally, salute garlic, great garlic, proof if anyone ever needed one that yes, there is a higher power.

Your Body—and Its Message

As a Slightly Older Guy, you know your strengths and weaknesses at the dinner table. Treat your stomach with respect but not servility. Cater to an occasional whim if you must—a slice of pepperoni pizza won't seriously shorten your life span—but don't cave in to a craving for fried calamari at bedtime. And if you lack the will to do so, take your antacids beforehand. Some of the new lemon-flavored ones are so satisfying you may end up forgetting all about the fried calamari.

The rules by now are evident: Don't eat while you're chasing a bus. Feel around for bones in your flounder. Shake the sand out of your spinach. When dining out, stick with the specialties. If a restaurant calls itself Davy Jones and has a photograph of a fish in the window, it's trying to tell you something. Don't order the corned beef and expect it to amount to much. Eat one meal at a time and don't start planning the next before you've gotten past the appetizer. Chew your food, of course, but don't forget to swallow it. And listen carefully to your body. If it asks for baked ziti, get some in there as soon as possible. The same is true of smelts. If it cries out for smelts, give it smelts. And don't accept any of the smelt substitutes.

There are many dining treats on the horizon, hundreds for all you know. Proceed cautiously, avoid jalapeño peppers, and there's no reason why you can't play out your hand in comfort as a well-fed Slightly Older Guy.

Earrings and Ponytails

There may be a cloud or two gathering up ahead, but that's all the more reason not to neglect your appearance. Only the truly discerning will be able to look past battered loafers and a jacket covered with soup stains to see the real you—which you may not want to reveal in any case.

"What about Albert Schweitzer?" you might ask. "He didn't care how *he* looked."

That may have been true of Schweitzer, but the chances are you're not going around collecting prizes and attending conferences on humanitarianism. If you are, then you might not care what you look like either. But remember, Schweitzer is said to have done poorly in cocktail lounges.

Forget Schweitzer. Concentrate on sprucing yourself up a bit.

The Great Earring Question

A question you might as well address right up front is whether you want to try an earring. At one time, this may have seemed an affectation, but now that accountants and captains of industry show up with them, you're liable to feel left behind if you don't pop one in.

A great fear has always been that if you wear one, someone is going to beat you up—but the very people who once concerned you are now parading around with earrings of their own, and starting to worry that you might beat *them* up.

If you decide to get an earring, the worst-case scenario—and it's not all that bad—is that you'll run into an unsavory type who's also wearing one. There may be some wary circling about in the street—you might Mace each other up a bit—but the chances are you'll go your separate ways, or who knows, even end up at the same party.

Once you've committed to wearing an earring, you'll have to decide which ear you want to put it on and exactly where on the ear you want it placed. It's no secret that the positioning of an earring can indicate sexual preference. But it can also signal anything from animal rights activism to support for the Tamil minority in Sri Lanka—and you might not have strong feelings about either cause. So do your research.

For starters, at least, you'll want to select an earring that's small and inconspicuous, although not so small that people will strain to see if it is indeed an earring or a pimple. Avoid giant tire-like affairs that are not only attention-getting but will also weigh you down to one side, potentially causing dizzy spells.

For your first public appearance, you can deal with your insecurity by either revealing the earring gradually, cupping one hand over it and giving peeks at it to an occasional passerby, or by storming into a waterfront bar, ordering a boilermaker, and flaunting it boldly at rowdies.

After several outings, you'll find it's become part of your look. Rarely will someone cry out, "Here comes the guy with the earring."

Once you've settled in comfortably as an earring person, there'll be a temptation to balance yourself off with a second earring—but this can lead to nose studs and metallic appendages on other body parts, and you may not want to go in that direction.

Stick with the one earring. Then give some thought to your hair.

Hair Today...

Hair plays a tremendous part in contemporary life. There's no question that Clinton's hair swung the election in his favor.* Does anyone doubt that Gorbachev would still be in power if it weren't for Yeltsin's great hair? You have to go back to Eisenhower to find a bald President, and that's because Adlai Stevenson had even less hair than Ike did.

Small wonder that the Slightly Older Guy is deeply concerned about his thinning and perhaps graying locks.

One way to deal with this is to use one of the many products that are designed to change your hair color overnight. If you're sensitive about trying one, you can always apply it in a small border town where no one knows you. If it doesn't work out or causes a stir, even in the small border town, just stay put for a month or so until it all grows out; then return home with your old hair and no one will be the wiser.

A toupee is another solution, but if you choose this option, make sure to stay with a top-of-the-line product and not just any old kind that's on sale at Woolworth's. Ask Tony Bennett where he got his. You don't want people poking each other and saying, "Did you see the rug on that guy?"

As to the rumor of a magazine in the works that "outs" bald people who wear hairpieces —there's no truth to it. You can relax on that score.

---

* Bush had hair, too, but it was that thin preppy kind which is not a vote-getter.

The Ponytail Decision

Inevitably, with the example of youth swirling all around you, you'll want to consider wearing your hair in a ponytail —assuming, of course, there's enough of it left. The Slightly Older Guy who grows a ponytail often does so in the hope of trimming years off his age, and with luck, being taken as the lead guitarist for Blind Melon. More specifically, a ponytail is designed to swing the focus away from your baldness, although this can backfire and call attention to your upper-back hair. Try to keep this unpleasant growth covered.

Ponytails are not appropriate for every profession. It's one thing for them to be mandatory at TriStar; it's quite another to imagine Secretary of State Warren Christopher wearing one as he strolls up to the microphone to announce a change in our stance toward Macedonia.

If you decide to go ahead with a ponytail, keep it at a modest length and neatly tied back with a rubber band. There have been tragic deaths involving commodities brokers who got their ponytails caught in elevator doors.

Above all, keep your hair clean. Nobody admires a Slightly Older Guy who looks like Howard Hughes.

A Wardrobe Update

With your earring and ponytail accounted for, you'll want to pay some attention to your wardrobe, which may be sadly out of date. A difficulty here for the Slightly Older Guy is that men's clothing never seems to wear out —with the exception of today's socks, which shrivel up into little balls after a use or two. Rather than discard a perfectly serviceable sports jacket, the Slightly Older Guy will stubbornly continue to wear it, even if it dates back to the Truman administration. At a certain point, however, you may decide—or the Board of Health may decide for you— to get rid of your old clothing, which may not be as easy as you think. Even the Salvation Army has to draw the line somewhere.

In pruning down your wardrobe, don't be overly aggressive. Keep in mind that certain items are capable of making a comeback. This has already happened in the case of Nehru jackets. And there's hope still for your collection of skinny ties.

The Slightly Older Guy "Look"

With space in your closets, you'll be ready to make a few modest purchases. But just because you haven't shopped for a while, there's no need to buy out the whole store. Some trousers and a jacket or two, deftly switched around in various combinations, can quietly establish you as a clotheshorse. Sometimes a single item can make a world of difference. A Versace tie, for example, with the right combination of fruit and palm trees painted on it, can result in crowds of the curious gathering around you at cocktail parties.

The bright side? As a Slightly Older Guy, you don't have to worry about wasting money on clothes that will "last you a lifetime."

The Well-Scrubbed Look

To secure your precarious footing as a Slightly Older Guy, you'll want to pay special attention to hygiene. Nose hairs should be trimmed off at the pass, and unless you play the guitar, you don't want to be seen with long fingernails. Although they are rarely credited with doing so, hairy ears have been known to choke off many a budding romance. So make sure to deal with that problem.

An entire industry exists to cope with your breath, so there's no excuse for any slip-up here. America has the best breath of any country, and you'll want to do your part in keeping it that way.

Soap, teeth whiteners, deodorants, wrinkle creams, moustache darkeners—they're all out there for you, and there's no excuse for not taking advantage of them. There are obstacles ahead—who could possibly argue with that? —but you'll be better able to face them as a well-groomed Slightly Older Guy.

At the Baseline

With your diet in order and your earring and ponytail in place, you want to make sure that you're a picture of fitness. As a Slightly Older Guy, you'll find that tennis is an excellent conditioner since it can be taken up at any time no matter how far along the road you've traveled. Benefits include a trim waistline and a belly that's been reduced in size so that there's no longer any need to disguise it with caftans. Time, unfortunately, may already have thinned out your legs; still, no matter how spindly they've become, some vigorous play on the tennis court should provide a bit of shape to them.

If you're a beginner, before you go charging out onto the courts it's advisable to invest in a lesson or two. There are a bewildering number of approaches to the game, and instructors vary wildly in their recommendations.

THE BALL

Some argue for making the ball the centerpiece of your game and keeping a watchful eye on it at all times. Others claim that watching it alone is of little value; what you want to do is make guesses as to its eventual whereabouts so that you can be on hand to greet it. Yet another school insists that it's not so much the ball that should be studied as it is your opponent's feet, although obviously not in lustful fascination.

THE NET

There's disagreement, too, as to what attitude to take toward the net, other than whacking it with your racket in frustration. Some recommend avoiding it at all costs; others encourage charging up to it fearlessly when given the slightest opportunity. A third group advocates approaching the net, though somewhat warily, and only after Building a Case, in the fashion of a prosecutor gathering evidence for an indictment.

Once the player has arrived at the net, however, there's a general consensus that the racket should be positioned so that it shields the genital area. Unsportsmanlike though it may appear, it's not unheard of for a diabolical opponent— in the hope of winning a match by default—to unleash a disabling shot in that direction.

STROKES

As for strokes in general, some advise lashing out with fury at every ball that comes your way. Others feel the wise course is to conserve energy, hitting the ball modestly until your opponent begins to tire and only then striking out with conviction. Players have been known to wait years for such an eventuality.

All schools agree that the novice should keep the ball in play long enough *to allow his opponent to be the one who commits the blunders*—and not leave the court in tears when this fails to happen.

As for particular strokes, you'll find instructors becoming lyrically extravagant in their advice on how to execute them. In attempting a backhand stroke, you'll be told to reach round in back of yourself and pull at the racket "as if you're unsheathing a bowie knife." As for the forehand, the trick is to swing through the ball and finish off the stroke by "shaking hands with yourself," although not necessarily in a congratulatory manner.

THE SERVE

The first serve is of great importance and should be delivered with authority. The second is another matter. Ideally, it should have some novelty to it, a coquettish little spin, for example, designed to overpower your opponent with its charm.

FEAR

After a number of lessons, you may experience a Fear of Actually Playing. But as a Slightly Older Guy, with time not necessarily working to your advantage, you need to get on with it. Put your lessons behind you and step out on the court, ready to do battle. Before doing so, it's essential that you have at the ready the most important weapon of all.

The Excuse for Poor Performance

As a Slightly Older Guy who's never played before, you're ideally situated in this regard. You can trot out on the court and declare in all candor, "I've just taken up the game." Or if you've played a bit as an undergraduate, heft the racket, look at it ruefully, and say, "Amazing. I haven't picked up one of these things in years."

Another successful gambit is to limp out on the court and say with a wince, "We can *try* a few points. I just hope the knee holds up."

The surface, too, can be blamed in advance as an excuse for poor play ("This is my first time on clay"), as can knavish behavior the night before ("If only I hadn't knocked back that last Stinger").

A morbid stratagem, in surprisingly wide use, is to whisper hoarsely, "That chemo sure takes a lot out of you."

Once you've announced your Excuse for Poor Performance, you can set about to play briskly, having stripped your opponent of any pride he might have taken in beating you. Should you score an upset victory, he'll have no choice but to slink away in humiliation.

Tennis Etiquette

Tennis etiquette is an important part of the game. When your opponent is preparing to serve, it's bad form to try to throw him off with cheap distractions ("Hold it right there, I see a gnat on your shoulder").

When the ball drops close to the line in the opposite court, it's your opponent's call as to whether it's in or out, and his judgment should be accepted graciously. Try not to be spiteful if you disagree with him ("Go ahead and *take* the point. Some of us aren't that desperate").

As a Slightly Older Guy, you'll be expected to behave decently in either victory or defeat. After a loss, you don't want to be seen skulking away, muttering dark threats of revenge. And should you win the match, there's no need for you to leap over the net in triumph, clap your opponent on the back, and say, "It could have gone either way." Nor is it attractive to follow the losing player into the locker room with a satisfied smirk. A simple handshake will suffice, or at most a sly wink, indicating that, after all, you *did* win the match.

Some Other Considerations

EQUIPMENT

Care should be taken in the selection of equipment, but with an understanding that eye-catching footwear and a racket that's been endorsed by Ivan Lendl are no substitutes for clean ground strokes. Courtesy requires, too, that you show up before each match with a new can of balls. Repeat-

edly saying "We might as well use yours" will quickly iden-
tify you as a cheapskate. And being spotted rooting around
in the shrubbery for used balls will only cause talk among
the other players.

PREPARATION

Stretching out before a match is a sound idea, as is tossing
back an aspirin or two as a means of fending off that
scourge of all tennis enthusiasts, the dreaded hamstring
pull. Worse than the injury itself is the player who'll stand
over your crumpled form and deliver a diagnosis: "I believe
you've popped your hammy."

A Little Respect

Be kind to your opponent. If he insists on winning every
point, let him go ahead and do so. As a Slightly Older
Guy, you've at least theoretically moved beyond such banal
concerns as winning or losing. You have the advantage of
knowing that the results of your match are not going to be
splashed all over *The New York Times,* pushing assaults on
Bosnia to the back pages. And there's no need to bear a
grudge against a victorious opponent. As a younger man,
you might have thought to yourself, "The little shit is going
to tell everyone he beat me." With the mantle of wisdom
on your shoulders, you can now sit back philosophically
and say to yourself, "So *what* if the little shit tells everyone
he beat me."

So go out there on the court, Slightly Older Guy, while
there's still time and you're still able. You'll experience a
sense of confidence and well-being, not overnight necessarily, but eventually, if you can just hang on long enough.

Some Other Roads
to Fitness

As a Slightly Older Guy, you're no doubt worried sick about not getting enough exercise—but this is not that bad. There is some evidence that worry itself, particularly among members of the Jewish faith,* can result in a lean and haggard look that often passes for fitness.

So don't worry about worrying.

Here are some other notions.

WALKING

If running, and even jogging, has become a strain, you might want to give some thought to walking. Call it "speed-walking" if it makes you feel better. Walking is obviously easier on the increasingly fragile knees, and there are circulatory benefits as well, particularly if the arms are swung out smartly, and away from the body, in the fascist style. (Don't overdo this or you'll set off counterdemonstrations by peace groups.)

WALKING AND RUNNING

There's no law that says you can't do both. That is, run a bit, walk when you get tired, then break into a run when you've rested up. Tell yourself that you're doing "wind sprints."

---

* Those who've been expecting "Slightly Older Goy" jokes are advised to look elsewhere.

Only the purists will object to this hybrid workout. ("Now see here. I've been watching you. Either walk or run, damnit.")

BIKING

Hazardous, of course, if you're dodging in and out of city traffic, but worth considering if you can get out to the countryside. You'll have to wear one of those ridiculous mushroom-shaped helmets that are mandatory in many areas. Factor in the fresh air, the scenery—and it's still excruciatingly boring. Try mixing it in with another more purposeful activity—such as delivering newspapers.

WORKOUT TAPES

An excellent means of getting off the ground in the morning. Be careful not to get caught up in Cindy Crawford's gyrations and forget to exercise.

AEROBICS

Best performed in classes, which are obviously a great place to meet women. Before dating a classmate, make sure you've seen her at least once when she's not in Spandex.

TREADMILLS, STAIRMASTERS

Here again, an activity that's stultifyingly dull. If you're determined to get on one of these machines, be sure to have some reading material. See to it that it's not too intriguing or you'll forget to get off.

This is an excellent way to get through Proust.

. . .

Take your exercise where and when you can. Leaping enthusiastically to your feet during exciting moments of a ball game can make for a nice little workout. Watching tennis matches from center court has been known to reduce neck fat.

"The Doctor Will See You Now"

If you're a representative Slightly Older Guy, you'll probably insist on being in the pink of condition before you see a doctor—and, of course, you'll be missing the point. The idea is not to impress the doctor with your health. If you show up when you're brimming over with vitality, there's very little he can do for you other than clap you on the shoulder and tell you to keep up the good work, which is hardly worth the money. So visit the doctor when there's something wrong with you. And don't worry about alarming him. No matter what you've come up with, the chances are he's run across a case or two of it before, perhaps in the tropics.

Credible Credentials

Under the new health-care reform, it's unlikely you'll get to see a doctor you want to be in the same room with, much less be treated by. But assuming you have a say in the matter, choose one who is not only competent but who is certified to practice medicine—and not just in the Andaman Islands. And if he's not affiliated with a reputable hospital, don't accept his explanation that he's been misunderstood —or that his only crime was that he tried too hard. Insist that he have a license.

Your best bet is to consult a doctor who is roughly your age and who won't be baffled by your condition.

If you're sitting on the examining table and you say, "Bet you've never seen anything like *this* before," the answer you want to hear is: "No, no. I've had it myself for years."

Older doctors tend to be conservative and won't recommend radical procedures when you stub your toe. But if you see one, make sure to inquire about *his* health. It can be discomforting to have a doctor die in your arms.

Women in Medicine

It's possible you've been shying away from doctors of the opposite sex because they're constructed differently and will be in the dark as to how your body functions. This is misguided. A female doctor can be counted on to have done her homework, and after all, at least a passing acquaintance with your anatomy is part of her job.

Ultimately, what you want is a doctor who shows up now and then and isn't away snorkeling when you feel your life is slipping away.

Just Testing

Preventive medicine is much in vogue and requires that you schedule an annual checkup (it can be tied in with the yearly inspection of your car). Some people see this as a needless expense, but one justification of the cost is that doctors are always going to find something wrong with you that will be covered, at least in part, by your medical insurance. You can make that a condition of the checkup if you like.

Tests will generally be ordered up, and they can be unnerving, although it isn't the tests themselves so much as waiting for the results that accounts for a considerable number of fatalities in America. Many a Slightly Older Guy has for his epitaph: "I'm still waiting for my test results." And when a report finally does roll in, there's a strong chance you'll get someone else's results, which may not always be a bad thing.

A favorite of many is the stress test, which amounts to not much more than a bracing little workout. There are Slightly Older Guys who sign up for the test as a substitute for jogging. Less appealing are CAT scans and MRI tests, which can be terrifying because of all the mysterious equipment. It's best to start with the familiar thermometer and blood pressure cuffs. As for the surrender of your body fluids, do it as graciously as possible.

There Goes the Arm

When it's finally sunk in that you're an official Slightly Older Guy, you may find yourself overreacting to the most trivial of symptoms. A slight swelling of the elbow and you'll be ready to say goodbye to your arm. At the onset of post-nasal drip, you'll find yourself dashing off a living will.

Even a clean bill of health won't appease you. If your doctor says you're in reasonably good health, don't panic and cry out, "What do you mean by 'reasonably'?" Of course, a slight touch of hypochondria is to be expected. Yet even in the case of the most robust Slightly Older Guy, a time will come when something really *has* gone amiss, which is why you'll find it useful to live near a hospital.

Pop in and say hello to the admitting personnel at the emergency room so they know you're friendly and won't be carrying an assault rifle if you're ever carted in. And if you have some spare time, work as a volunteer, not only to help the unfortunate but to build up some goodwill in case you ever need to be resuscitated. Additionally, see if you can get a Fast-Track card so that if you pound a nail into your palm, you can be whisked right through and won't have to spend a weekend filling out forms.

Get in and out of these places as fast as possible. If you're ever forced actually to stay in a hospital, make sure that you have an escape plan worked out, so that you can slip away in case anyone tries to do something to you.

Do-It-Yourself Medications

Overall, you'll want to stay as far away as you can from hospitals and doctors; once you get involved with them, there's no telling where it can lead. When something's not quite right, very often the best treatment is to pop an aspirin and take a nap. Aspirin is every bit the wonder drug it's cracked up to be, although a great deal of pressure has been put on it—and you can't, for example, expect it to function as a knee replacement.

Don't look down at home remedies. Chicken soup, for example, has proven healing powers provided the chickens were raised in a good barn. Cranberry juice is excellent for the urinary tract, although it may keep your lips in a pucker. Mustard is effective in clearing out the sinus passages, and Grey Poupon will clear them out permanently. For warding off colds, there's always a clove of garlic, which is even more effective when taken with veal marsala.

If It's Long Life You're After

Health, it will become increasingly clear, is more important than stocks and bonds, even when they're in medical supplies. And illness is a great equalizer. If disaster strikes, your lofty status isn't going to do you much good. When your doctor tells you you're a very sick man, don't say, "There must be some mistake. I'm the assistant merchandising director of Allied Chemical." You're just not going to get any points for that. If the Sultan of Bahrain comes down with Kunstler's syndrome, he's in the same boat as the poor man who holds the door for him, although it's true that he can send for Kunstler and see how *he* deals with it.

Much of what happens is out of your hands. If Schreiber's knee has been in the family for years, there's a chance you'll get a dose of it, and the best you can do is hold the line at one knee. It's fairly clear that common sense and not panic is the key to longevity. Stay out of the rain, don't let anyone sneeze at you, and remember that constant worry about your health is the quickest path to the grave. Let someone else worry about it. Marry a nurse. And above all, keep busy. The Slightly Older Guy who is always dashing off to seminars doesn't have *time* to get sick. And if you do come down with something, remember, there are worse things —such as an IRS audit.

Two Sinful Pursuits

SMOKING

Although a great many Slightly Older Guys have given up cigarettes, still others continue to puff away with abandon. Some do so in morbid defiance of death, considering each inhalation a little attention-getting challenge to their mortality. Others take a Clintonesque stance, saying they don't inhale, hoping against hope that the tobacco companies are right and that smoking is just a harmless and amusing pastime. The Slightly Older Guy, too, might claim that he came of age at a time when film stars couldn't wait to finish their (offstage) love-making so they could blow clouds of smoke at each other. Or he'll remind you that it was impossible to be taken seriously as a person of worldly substance unless your eyes were pained and squinted and there was a cigarette dangling from your lips.

Dollars and Sense

"I've tried everything and I can't stop," the Slightly Older Guy might say in frustration. "I guess I'm just a smoker to the end."

Not necessarily. There's always the appeal of economic self-interest—which is generally the cause of wars, revolutions, and most human behavior. Try calculating the amount of money you've spent on cigarettes over the last year—or over the past decade, for that matter—and you might find the figure alarming. There are Slightly Older Guys who believe they've come into a mysterious financial windfall, with coins spilling out of their pockets, before they realize their good fortune began the day they gave up smoking.

The Old Dazzle

When the above tactic doesn't work, you might, in a last-ditch effort to lose the habit, try appealing to your vanity.

There's an obligation to report here—with some reluctance—that the teeth begin to yellow a bit in the natural aging process. This, combined with smoking, can result in a gray and grungy look about the mouth, desirable perhaps in the resident poet at Swarthmore but unappetizing in the case of the average Slightly Older Guy.

The good news here is that there is a new process* that, in roughly two weeks' time, can whiten your teeth, add some sparkle to them, and virtually restore the smile you had in your college yearbook photo. The bad news is that this remarkable process will reverse itself if you continue to smoke.

So the choice is yours. Do you return to the habit that secretly made you cringe with embarrassment and has obviously put you on a downhill slide? Or do you go forth with the killer smile that once impressed cheerleaders and never failed to cause a stir at parties? Slightly Older Guys who've chosen the latter option report having a new bounce in their step—and are somewhat puzzled about why they ever smoked in the first place.

DRINKING

As a Slightly Older Guy, you might consider yourself a moderate drinker, a fellow who knocks back a cocktail or two

* Night White.

in order to sharpen your appetite and make the world seem a bit more agreeable. And you've no doubt been heartened by the medical finding that drinking, when held in check, helps guarantee a long and robust life.

"That's me, all right," you might point out. "I'll have one or two to steel myself for Peter Jennings and the evening news. After that, you can't sell me a drink."

No one says you have to give up this pleasurable activity. But if your evenings have been passing by in a blur and you can vaguely recall any of the following situations, it may be that you're no longer, strictly speaking, just a moderate drinker:

- You make nightly calls to the White House, demanding an invasion of Canada.

- You can't remember your phone number.

- Several mornings a week, you wake up on lawns.

Sound familiar? Then you might want to have a look at what it is—and how much of it—you've been drinking. Let's face it, a pint-sized tumbler of Old Rotgut amounts to more than a harmless little pick-me-up. And the chances are you don't even recollect all the brandy and wine that followed. As a Slightly Older Guy, your memory has already taken a pounding. Give it a break.

When you're a Slightly Older Guy, you'll also discover that, through some quirk of body chemistry, one drink now does the work of four. Unfortunately, the same principle holds true for hangovers, which can no longer be waved off with a nap and a cup of coffee. You've got to account for a full day or two before you're back on your feet—which are not all that steady to begin with.

Part Three

Affairs of
the Heart

A Circle of Friends

From the day it sinks in that you are, indeed, a
Slightly Older Guy, it's essential that you surround yourself
with a supportive group of old friends. Rounding them up
may not be as easy as you might think. Some, you'll find,
are being maintained on Prozac and are afraid to leave the
house. Others will have moved to remote parts of the globe,
such as Kansas City. A few may want to have nothing more
to do with you. If any remain, it's important to treasure
them and to forgive them their minor transgressions. If a
friend occasionally cries out, "You've always been a selfish
bastard," take him aside, humor him gently, and try to put
his outbursts in perspective. Maybe there's some truth to
the charge. Assure him that in the future you'll go out of
your way not to be a selfish bastard. If he continues to
denounce you at large public gatherings, you have every
right to question his loyalty.

The Slightly Older Guy who feels that he's friendless and
alone may have a wide variety of opportunities staring him
in the face and not realize it.

Some examples:

THE ENDODONTIST

Don't disqualify your endodontist as a potential friend just
because he's spent years plugging up your root canals.

Without his mask, and away from his gas delivery system, he may come off as an entirely different person.

Invite him on a fishing trip. Once you've fried your catch and are lying beneath the stars, sound him out on his hopes and fears and dreams, not just for a better America but for the future of root canal work. He may turn out to be a wonderful new friend. In this same spirit, you might want to take a fresh look at your accountant. Invite him to a concert. If the evening doesn't work out, you can always write it off.

THE OPPOSITE SEX

It may be that you haven't been paying sufficient attention to women in the context of friendship. You may not know it, but women are the best confidantes and will guard your secrets from all but their closest girlfriends. Then, too, they can be counted on to give you the very latest information on What Women Want. And the fact that a female friend will outlive you by an average of seven years means she'll be around to speak highly of you when you're gone.

And remember: in forging friendships with women, try to keep sex out of it unless it's absolutely necessary. But if sex does work its way in, you may find yourself with that most remarkable of all combinations—a lover *and* a friend.

MAN'S BEST FRIEND

Dogs are completely nonjudgmental, and that quality alone makes them the most loyal of companions. If you're forced to commit an ax murder in your dog's presence, he'll turn the other way, as long as he's fed on time. Remember, however, that friendship with a dog does have its limits. You may be able to share your innermost thoughts and feelings with a schnauzer, but you can't expect him to reciprocate.

FAIR-WEATHER FRIENDS

If you find yourself a little short of friends, it may be that you've set your standards too high.

"Sven will never make *my* list," you might say snappishly. "He's a fair-weather friend."

Perhaps that's true, but at least Sven is around in fair weather. Which is more than you can say for your enemies. Not every friend can be counted on to nurse you back to health when you come down with a cold. Or lend you his Harley-Davidson. And it's only the rare friend who'll rush over with a howitzer when you're having a boundary dispute with your neighbor.

Lighten up. Don't insist that your friends be of the highest moral fiber. Many a fascinating evening has been spent with an acquaintance who's under indictment and has to wear electronic leg irons.

OLDER FRIENDS

To the extent that they exist, try to cultivate a circle of friends who are even older than you are. Their concerns may be a little downbeat—Successful Bypasses, Interactive Walkers, the Joy of Dying in Your Sleep—but they'll provide you with some idea of what's in your not-so-distant future. As the youngest member of such a group, your only responsibility will be to sit back and listen, murmuring an occasional "That was way before my time." You'll come away feeling like a pup and looking, by comparison, like a Slightly Younger Guy.

WIVES

Fortunate is the Slightly Older Guy who can count his wife as a friend.

"I don't need anyone else," you might declare, perhaps with a little smugness. "Not when I have Megan at my side."

It's important to be honest here. Megan may be a wonderful woman, but has she always been at your side? What about the time when the cucumber slice was stuck in your throat and Megan wouldn't stop watching *All My Children?* Wasn't it the FedEx man who administered the Heimlich maneuver?

No disrespect for Megan, but why saddle her with the responsibilities of friendship? She has enough trouble being a wife.

DON'T BE A STRANGER

The rules of friendship are far from rigid, but you do have to make contact once in a while.

"Carl and I don't *have* to speak," you might say in rebuttal. "Our friendship is beyond that."

That may be true, but do you have to let thirty years go by before calling him? Carl might be an entirely different person now. Maybe he's had a sex change. There might not even *be* a Carl anymore. So pick up the phone. And don't start wondering why he hasn't called you. He may not have *heard* about your gallbladder. Or maybe he lost your number. Isn't it possible that Carl has fallen on hard times and can't afford a long-distance call?

Life's too short—just give the man a ring.

Ingredients of Friendship

- A good friend will care about your well-being. Pinching at your hip fat and saying, "Gained a few pounds there, haven't we, fella?" is not a genuine display of concern.

- The stalwart friend can be counted on to show up at important milestones in your life, ranging from birthday parties to jury trials for insider trading.

- A good friend will have a eulogy prepared well in advance of your funeral—as you'll no doubt have one on hand for his. (It's not useful to speculate morbidly on who'll get to deliver his speech first.)

- Wealth should not be held against a friend as long as he's prepared to hand some of it over now and then. Nor should fame stand in the way of camaraderie. The Slightly Older Guy, with a secure sense of himself, will think nothing of inviting Kevin Costner into his inner circle.

A Great *Friend*

Wives may come and go, children leave home, but a true friend is in it for the long haul. Short of being thrown out of the house, he'll remain at your side until the closing curtain. And losing a friend is a grave matter indeed, not to be put in the same category as a lost sweater. A true friendship takes years to develop. You can't spend a night on the town with a Florida real estate speculator you met at a bar and expect him to take the place of Doodles McKenzie, whom you've known since grade school.

The ideal friend will say little, chuckle amiably at familiar anecdotes, and not repeat attacks on your character that he's overheard in the locker room of your club. He'll be responsive to your changing moods. You may have been relying on one friend for discussions of William Gaddis novels and another for company at topless mud-wrestling events, but the ideal friend will happily accommodate both tastes.

As a Slightly Older Guy, you may decide one night to stop worrying about friends, your own company is all you'll ever need. Having arrived at that conclusion, simply take

yourself to a hockey game. Eventually, however, you'll discover that there is no substitute for a real friend—ideally
one who's on the homely side and can always be counted
on to be in worse shape than you are.

Divorce—and the Ex-Wife

As a Slightly Older Guy, there's a good chance
you've been divorced and have an ex-wife or two floating
about somewhere. This is not a particularly pleasant situation to contemplate. An ex-wife conjures up thoughts of
What Might Have Been, the sheer waste of it, the monstrous
legal fees that could so easily have been diverted to other
causes and pastimes, such as the pursuit of your present
wife. And the financial pain that followed your divorce. Not
that she's to blame. No one doubts her need for support.
But once her ostrich farm began to thrive, surely she could
have returned an alimony payment or two. Just as a token
of gratitude.

As it happens, there's no such thing as divorce. You may
have a legal document that *says* you've been set free, but the
memories—bittersweet if you're lucky—continue to form a
bond. If there are children in the picture, you're bound to
be flung together, at a son's engagement, a daughter's folk-
singing debut. Years may have passed, but there's always
one more document to be signed, and there continue to be
grounds for a case, however weak, of spousal abuse. You
may have already formulated your defense: "Hey, listen, *I'm*
not the one who hired a hit man."

A Game Plan

What's to be done about it? As little as possible. It's probably better to let sleeping dogs lie. Plan a sociable lunch if

you like, but keep it at the planning stage. If you go forward with the idea, a single unfortunate reference will inevitably cause voices to be raised and drinks flung in your face. It's possible to remain in civilized touch with an ex-wife, but only in the world of Noël Coward.

Approach all phone calls warily. They'll start off pleasantly enough, but there's always going to be a dark subtext, generally a costly one. Rare is the ex-wife who calls just to see how you're getting along.

The key to amiable coexistence on the same planet is to stay out of her life—and hope she stays out of yours. Don't even wonder what she's up to. With luck, she will have remarried. If she's remained unattached, resist the impulse to send a friend out there to court her. She didn't care for you. Why would she like him?

Perhaps she was your first love, but that may as well have been in Precambrian times. Think of the experience as having helped make you a seasoned Slightly Older Guy.

Your ex-wife knew you when you thought nothing of punching out headwaiters and taking naps on highway dividers with a bottle of Jack Daniel's as a pillow. There's no need for her to know how civilized you've become.

Wish your ex-wife well. Tell her you hope that she lives to be one hundred and has a rich, fulfilling life in Winnipeg.

The Slightly Older Wife

Fortunate is the Slightly Older Guy who has some-
how managed to stay married—even though he now has a
Slightly Older Wife.

There are great advantages to being in this situation.
Companionship, shared experiences, an acceptance of your
many eccentricities, the willingness to overlook snores and
gargling sounds that might prove unappealing to a younger
mate. Someone to assist you if you've slipped on an an-
chovy. Communication in shorthand, especially in the bed-
room, where a single codeword such as *scissors* or
fleaflicker is all that's required in assuming a favored inti-
mate position.

With a Slightly Older Wife as a companion, there's no
need to fill up silences with idle chitchat.

With luck, you may not have to talk at all.

Words of Caution

Along with the comforts of having a Slightly Older Wife,
there are also areas of great sensitivity that are best not
ignored.

Here are some advisories:

• Endearments such as "sweet old thing" and
"good old gal," no matter how well
intentioned, are bound to be taken in the

wrong spirit—and should be held to a
minimum.

• If a few gray hairs show up on your Slightly
Older Wife's head, don't be the first to point
them out ("Aha, what have we here?"). The
chances are she's already spotted them. Then,
too, humming "The Old Gray Mare" is not
reassuring.

• Don't try to justify the hiring of an attractive
young assistant by pointing to her exceptional
background and the dent she's going to put in
your workload. Hire a plain-looking young
woman and hope there are hidden fires
burning within her.

• Pay strict attention to birthdays and
anniversaries, even if this requires nailing up
poster-sized reminders in your office. Make
sure that gifts are thought out carefully and
are personal in nature. Black & Decker tool
kits will not be appreciated. In this area, a
sudden, unannounced gift, for no particular
purpose, will put you in good standing for
some time to come—and won't necessarily
indicate that you've started having an affair.

• If your Slightly Older Wife lies about her age,
don't correct the error. Let it slide. That'll
make her less likely to correct you when you
tell a friend, "Oh, I only put on about four or
five pounds."

• When a Slightly Older Wife parades in with an
outrageous new hairstyle—and you hadn't

noticed anything wrong with the old one—
tell her she reminds you of a young Greta
Garbo.

- Your sex life may have become subdued and
even "cozy," but there's no need to point this
out at every turn. Should a Slightly Older Wife
exhibit a sudden burst of sexuality, rein in
your surprise ("What's gotten into you?") and
try to keep up with her.

- Don't sulk if her career has blazed on ahead
of yours. Count your blessings, tidy up the
house, and hope she likes what you've fixed
for dinner.

- Include her in your vacation plans. The idea
of tooling around Amsterdam unencumbered
may seem appealing, but remember, you're a
Slightly Older Guy now, amorous adventures
are few and far between, and you'll probably
end up sightseeing all by yourself.

Care, concern, respect—those are the watchwords. A
Slightly Older Wife has invested heavily in you, however
rashly. This has put her in the same boat as you are, and
after all this time you might as well sail off into the sunset
together.

And Under No Circumstances

Never confess an adultery, no matter how long it's been buried in the past. In a Ferenc Molnár story, a ninety-year-old man tells his ninety-year-old wife of an affair he had with her friend, fifty years back. With her two remaining teeth, she bites off the tip of his nose.

The Slightly Older Guy
and His Kids

Here are some thoughts for the Slightly Older Guy about his children:

- Don't be disappointed if your son doesn't follow in your footsteps. Grit your teeth and try to be encouraging. At some later date, he may decide to give up the tattoo parlor and join you in dentistry.

- It's not a betrayal if a son or daughter doesn't share your taste in music. Not all teenagers are drawn to Perry Como.

- Even if you suspect that a son or daughter isn't really yours, don't banish the kid from your affections. It's possible to learn to love a child who is growing up to closely resemble your accountant.

- If your mature son decides to move out of the house, don't grab him by the lapels and beg him to stay. Say goodbye graciously and enjoy the free time you have until he moves back.

- Child-rearing is expensive, and it's naïve to think you'll get back every penny of your

investment. Remember, you spent all that
money out of love. If a child succeeds in the
world and wants to reward you with a
personal Gulfstream jet, grab it before he
changes his mind and gives it to his mother.

• It's natural to continue to think of sons and
daughters as your kids, even when they're
heading up multinational conglomerates. But
try to draw the line at age forty.

• Sex continues to be a delicate area in the
rearing of children. Give it a great deal of
thought before turning the whole business
over to your wife. (Then when your kids start
having kids, you can safely assume they've got
the hang of it.)

• If your daughter shows up with a potential
mate who's clearly not the rocket scientist you
had in mind, hide your feelings and try to be
a good sport about it. Keep in mind that your
future father-in-law didn't exactly faint with
delight when you appeared on the scene.

• Inevitably, your Slightly Older Kid is going to
have a child of his own. He'll generally
announce the event with a chilling midnight
call: "Guess what? I'm presenting you with a
grandchild." When someone addresses you as
"Grandpa," you'll probably be unamused at
first, whipping your head around and saying,
"I beg your pardon . . ." But Cary Grant got
used to it. You can, too. At the extreme, you
might even wind up with one of those
bumper stickers that say defiantly:

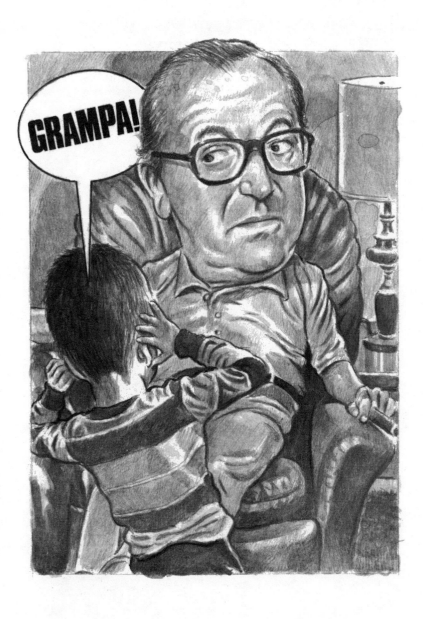

"Grandparent—and proud of it." And there's
no question you'll grow to love the new
member of the team, racing out to Minnesota
once a month to make sure he's getting his
share of pony rides.

Dating—and the Eleventh-Hour Romance

With the clock ticking at a maddening pace, the Slightly Older Guy who has been triumphant as a bachelor may suddenly panic at the thought of finding himself stranded in the late innings with no comforting hand to see him through. There are practical matters to consider. What if he falls down the stairs in the middle of the night and there's no one standing by to cart him off to the hospital? Or does he really want to tour the Greek islands as a solitary passenger, staring out at the Aegean, with no one to share his reflections on antiquity?

If you find yourself in this position—or if you're a Slightly Older Guy who is newly divorced—you may be a bit shaky when it comes to the rituals of romance. But there's no reason to rush off an application for a mail-order bride. Nor trust your fate to a computer dating service. Available women can be found close to home and in the most mundane of settings. The supermarket, for example, is generally teeming with prospects. An amusing remark at the checkout counter to an attractive fellow shopper can lead to the most rewarding of liaisons ("I see we're both Boar's Head ham enthusiasts").

The post office, too, is brimming with possibilities. And here again, a clever off-hand comment ("How about those new Elvis commemoratives!") may very well yield romantic dividends.

Some Interesting Candidates

Laundromats are generally filled with comely young Irish wenches, just in from County Cork and looking for a sponsor, ideally a Slightly Older Guy with a spare room. Bookstores, too, have become a magnet for serious-minded women with romance on their agenda. Particularly appealing are those clustered around the Isak Dinesen shelves. And there's no need to turn your nose up at topless dancers, assuming that a supple and exposed body is a sign of meager intelligence. By day, a surprising number are enrolled at the NYU film school. Others are hard at work on Willa Cather theses. In fact, it's not uncommon to run across a stripper who's a wizard at molecular biology.

Vintage Material

The Slightly Older Guy who has spent most of his years swinishly dating younger women will discover an entirely new world when he hooks up with a contemporary. Shared recollections of John Foster Dulles and Nelson Eddy are certain to be enlivening. Proceeding more boldly in this direction, you might even consider taking up with a woman who is considerably older than you are. If you decide to head this way, try for a grande dame type who's spent a great deal of her time in Paris and palled around with Anaïs Nin.

An Assortment of Other Choices

A good many Slightly Older Guys have begun to target nurses, not only for their romantic potential but as a means of setting up an in-house alternative to the Clinton health plan. There's no need to stalk the corridors of hospitals in search of prospects, but if you happen to be paying a death-bed visit to an old colleague, there's no harm in taking a good look at the nurse who's seeing him through—and don't forget to take note of the quality of her work.

Actresses, as is commonly known, are cheerful and attractive companions, but they're away on location a good deal of the time, making them vulnerable to affairs with Keanu Reeves. Particularly interesting are Women Who Tag Along at Dinner Parties. Many are wounded creatures, haunted and star-crossed. Others are fresh and spirited and open to challenge. In any case, there's something captivating about a tag-along. You'll find yourself wanting to see to it that she never has to tag along again.

In casting about for a romantic teammate, try not to be taken in by a single characteristic—a passing resemblance to Deborah Norville, for example, or an imitation of Julio Iglesias doing bird calls, which is bound to pale on repetition. And don't be taken in by a British accent, which can make the most routine comment sound Shakespearean. "I'll just pop into the loo" sounds eloquent on the lips of a rascal just in from Sheffield, but doesn't really add up to much when its content is examined closely.

A Word of Caution

Be wary of women who toss their hair a lot. It's difficult to build something lasting on this one attribute. And remember that chronic hair-tossing can lead to serious neck injury.

The Opening Gambit

"All right, all right," you say. "I'll take your word for it. Maybe there are women all over the place. So what if I spot one? How do I get the thing started?"

For openers, there's no need to lie about your age. On the other hand, you don't have to be overly forthright about it, either ("I'm Todd Mullins and guess what—I'm fifty-two"). Nor do you want to come on too forcefully by boasting about your accomplishments. Hold off for a bit before announcing that you're head of the neighborhood improvement association.

Salt in your credits slowly and gracefully. Do the same with your marital history. You want to avoid kicking off a new friendship with the story of your two divorces and the many shortcomings of your former wives.

Very often, the best opening remark is simple and direct. "How are you tonight?" is a perfectly acceptable ice-breaker —unless, of course, it's daytime.

Your Next Move

Fortunate is the Slightly Older Guy who has a romance that's briskly under way. But he'll soon have to make up his mind as to whether he wants to Live Together with his new companion—or push ahead to what, in many cases, will be a second or even third try at marriage. The former is a precarious arrangement; since either partner is free to light out at a moment's notice, it involves a certain amount of walking on eggs. As to the more secure alternative, the Slightly Older Guy who's been round the marital horn before will want to proceed with particular caution. With time in short supply, the last thing he needs for his end game is another bitter face-off in divorce court—this time with Raoul Felder.

There is no need to tick off the many criticisms that have been directed at marriage. We all know what they are, and of course, confinement generally heads the list. Yet in the teeth of this, there are Slightly Older Guys who insist it's marriage that's always afforded them the greatest degree of freedom.

"I'm so free that I don't *have* to have affairs."

If this is freedom, then so be it.

The Swan-Song Affair

In quite another situation is the Slightly Older Guy who's been comfortably married for a decade or so but feels there's something missing in his life.

"It's not Tanya," he might say. "Tanya's great and I guess I love her. She's my best friend and we get on decently enough in bed. And yet . . ."

And yet: the two plaintive words that generally signal a yearning for an Eleventh-Hour Romance—and the despondent feeling that the Slightly Older Guy is fated not to experience one. Never again the stolen kiss in a taxi, the anxious phone call, the inevitable theme song, the dizziness, the anticipation, the damp and sultry consummation on a hot night in August in the empty city.

"How I'd love to have another one of those," the Slightly Older Guy might lament. "And if I can't, I might as well pack it in."

If these are your true feelings, there's no point in casting about aimlessly for a love affair. But inevitably, in the course of a normal life, one is bound to creep up on you with little warning. A handshake, the merest glance, and there it is, having come into being in mystery and silence, like a virus.

The question then becomes one of whether to go forward in madness, ignoring Tanya's years of devotion and all that you've built together in Armonk. And this is not to mention little Tanya. Do you turn your back on her as well?

Don't delude yourself by thinking that you can keep any of this from the instinctively brilliant Tanya herself. She's bound to guess the instant you present her with the guilt-scented bouquet ("You're seeing another woman, aren't you? Why, Budd, why?").

The wisest move at this point—as if wisdom has anything to do with it—is to do and say as little as possible, and to retreat for a brief period from Tanya as well as the object of your infatuation. If you can manage it, spend a week alone, perhaps on an Indian reservation, allowing your passions to cool—and assuring Tanya with repeated phone calls that you're spending all your time placing bets on Keno. At the end of your trip, you may well decide to plunge ahead and tear your life to shreds by starting what's left of it anew with your fresh discovery.

But remember, it's late in the day, and there's always the risk of botching the whole business and eventually ending up with neither Tanya nor her replacement in a rooming house in Santa Monica, alone with your liver spots. The saner course is to accept your loss and remain with Tanya —if she'll take you back.

"I've had it with love," you might declare if Tanya has washed her hands with you, wondering if the sentiment might not catch fire as a country-western lyric.

And then, just as you've resigned yourself to a joyless, loveless, humdrum existence, you might attend a function one night and catch a glimpse across the buffet table of a slender form, an intriguing profile, a heartbreaking cascade of silken hair, all of it capped off by a throaty and engaging laugh.

"Oh my God," you think, caught off-guard, reeling. "Who *is* she? I've got to meet her."

Then she turns—and it's Tanya.

A Young Wife

If you're an unattached Slightly Older Guy, you may have toyed with the idea of taking a young wife. Assuming there's one available, you'll find that there are many attractive features to this option. Heads will turn when you enter restaurants, roués will lift their glasses in admiration, and only on occasion will some spoilsport be overheard whispering, "What on God's earth is she doing with him?"

There will be an assumption that you're quite a virile fellow and that power and money are yours as well, when in actuality you may have a total of four hundred dollars in the bank.

Using your young wife as a beard, you'll be able to slip into Lemonheads concerts.

Challenged to keep up with a youthful bride, you'll find yourself performing feats of strength you thought were beyond you—such as lifting couches and, in a more playful vein, lifting your young wife as well.

At nightclubs, she'll drag you out onto the dance floor and encourage you to gyrate wildly with the music. And if you don't keep up, you'll be bumped off the floor, the sound of "Gramps" echoing in your ears.

Some Other Perks

Along with a young wife will come a whole group of young friends, and it's entirely possible that several may ask to hide out in your apartment for a few months. A completely new family will come along as part of the package, too, and you can't assume that all will be the salt of the earth. Some time may have to be set aside for visiting an aunt or two in institutions.

A young wife will see you as a mentor and will listen attentively as you fill her in on the defense of Stalingrad. All your stories will be fresh to her ("Tell me one more time about the night you met Senator Al D'Amato at a fundraiser"), and you will be surprised to find that you tell them with a new verve.

As a young person, she probably hasn't seen all that much of the world, and you can look forward to her high excitement when she's taken to Manhattan and shown the Chrysler Building.

No request for sexual pleasure will be denied, even when you wish it would be. (For an expansion of this theme, see section on "Sex and the Slightly Older Guy.") You may, on occasion, long for the company of someone who remembers Ed Meese, but there are treats in store that will easily compensate for this minor void in your life. For example, a young wife will expose you to an entirely new approach to the English language ("Like don't you think this place is like totally cool?").

A Few Drawbacks

There's no question that a young wife will lift your spirits, but there are some disadvantages to the arrangement that must be considered. For all of her tender years, she may require extensive dental work. And there may have been a brief earlier marriage that somehow slipped her mind—to someone named "Whalebone" who keeps showing up and asking for money to tide him over until he lands another bartender job.

Coming as she does from a more recent generation, a

young wife will tend to be more concerned about the planet than you are and could very well hold you personally responsible for the California water shortage. You may find she has stationed herself outside the bathroom door to time your showers and listen for extra flushes. In fact, if you've been counting on a double income, you may be unpleasantly surprised to learn that she's taken on an unpaid job with Friends of the Ozone Layer.

As a Slightly Older Guy, your taste in dining will no doubt have taken on some sophistication, and here, too, there can be trouble. With little interest in this pleasurable activity, a young wife may be puzzled by your lack of enthusiasm as she sets before you for dinner a Coke and a platter of onion rings. With your own digestive system becoming increasingly shaky, you'll wonder how one person can polish off all those chimichangas and still look so good.

She'll need much more sleep than you do, and as a result you may not see much of her during the daytime. As to the evening hours, she'll no doubt be much more attached to television than you are—and you might find yourself competing with Letterman for her attention.

An Addition to the Team

Inevitably, a young wife will make it known that motherhood is her ultimate goal in life. This need will be communicated by a certain look in her eyes, a newfound interest in all things related to infants, or a sudden anguished Medea-like cry in a crowded elevator: *"I want a baby!"*

After you've made your apologies to the other passengers and ushered her outside, it might be a good idea to take this need of hers seriously. It doesn't matter that you've already produced three or four guitar players and turned them loose on the world—she hasn't, and it is probably wise to indulge her.

However, you'll find there's more to it this time around

than just muddling through a good part of the following year and showing up at the hospital with cigars. Expecting a child means signing on for Lamaze classes, and as the senior member of the group you'll probably be the one chosen to play the part of the vulva. Extensive instruction will follow on the timing of contractions. Although you've been described as a coach, you'll be expected to do more during the delivery than holler "Way to go, babe!" It's entirely possible your wife will be so zonked out during much of the procedure that *you're* the one who'll be asked questions such as "Shall we shoot for an epidural?" It's useful to have an intelligent response prepared—and not simply wave casually and tell the doctor, "It's your dime."

"It's a Girl"

You can expect your new family member to blend into the household without too much disruption for a while, but become more conspicuous as time rolls along. It is important to remember here that you're a Slightly Older Guy. If you've come up with another son, an invitation to "shoot a few hoops" may be enough to send you packing off for a new life in Central Europe.

A daughter is another matter. Once you've calmed down and stopped running joyously and idiotically through the streets, you'll want to establish some rules, the most important of which is: No Dating Until Forty. Then it's simply a matter of laying down weaponry to discourage prospective suitors and learning to say "No." This, as you might guess, is not an easy task. There have been isolated reports of fathers turning down a daughter's request, but none can be verified.

Through all of this, be sure not to neglect your wife, who's still young (although not as young as your daughter). Both will need to be indulged, which can be expensive as you'll notice when the monthly Gap bills come rolling in.

Pets will undoubtedly be added to the family mix, and they are costly as well.

Nonetheless, you'll see such expenditures as a small price to pay as you settle down in your new life: a Slightly Older Guy with a young wife, a daughter, a Japanese temple dog, several cats, and a macaw.

Part Four

Affairs of the Pocketbook

Some Small and Painless Economies

It's not unreasonable to think that after years of slaving away as a gazebo salesman, you'd have a little something in the bank to show for it. But that isn't always the case. Take a cold, hard look at your finances. After factoring in mortgage payments, credit card charges, outstanding loans, and a few old plumbing bills, it may turn out that you have a net worth of $164 in cash. Or maybe you're $164 in the red. In either case, it's never too late to economize, even if you're a Slightly Older Guy.

Here are some thoughts on how to do so.

FORGET BRAND-NAME PRODUCTS

There's very little difference between generic ketchup and the real thing. You'll note, too, that your dog is just as happy wolfing down biscuits that come in a box with a plain label. Just don't let him in on it. As for aspirin, a generic tablet will get rid of most of your headache, if not all of it. And you don't have to buy generic products in an alleyway from someone named Lightning. They're available in major retail outlets and are generally kept over on the side somewhere.

SCALE DOWN YOUR OPERATION

If your income has fallen from $100,000 a year to, say, $4,750, it may be time to reconsider whether you really need a bookkeeper, an accountant, a lawyer, and a public relations adviser. Why keep on paying a financial planner when there's nothing to plan? Take on some of these functions yourself. Call it down-sizing if it makes you feel better. Apply the same theory to your living quarters. If you've been keeping up a twelve-room house for some weird romantic reason ("It's where I want to die"), think about the fact that maintaining a huge house is one of the leading causes of death. Consider getting a smaller place. You don't have to go to the other extreme and rent a broom closet in Toledo. Just get something comfortable.

STOP REACHING FOR THE CHECK

Let someone else pick up the tab for a change. If a woman offers to pay for your dinner, don't wrestle her to the ground in an attempt to pry the check away from her. Let her pay the damned thing. You'll not only save a few bucks, you'll also help her to consolidate her hard-fought gains over the last decade.

Should this new, tight-fisted style make you less popular, you can always find new friends at church socials.

SCALE BACK YOUR TIPPING

And be a bit more selective about it. It's one thing to tip the waiter, but do you have to tip the owner of the restaurant, too? And the head of the chain? Of course not. They're doing just fine.

"But what about Sinatra?" you might ask. "He throws around hundred-dollar bills, and look at all the respect *he* gets."

To begin with, you're not Sinatra. Can you sing "My Way" with half the emotion he puts into it? Are you being paid $100,000 a night by Caesars and getting a big round of applause as you're carted away after fainting on stage? Forget Sinatra. Just go about your business and do it your way.

LOOK FOR "GOING OUT OF BUSINESS" SALES

Don't howl with laughter when you see an "Everything Must Go" sign in a store window and assume it's just a come-on. Some stores really *do* go out of business, and when they do, they give away merchandise at virtually bargain prices. But before you make a purchase, check with the owner and make sure he's *really* destitute.

PUMP YOUR OWN GAS

If someone sees you doing it, it's not as if you've been caught in a bordello. Many outstanding Americans now pump their own gas and are just as embarrassed about it as you are. It's an excellent way to get some fresh air, save a little money, and strike back at the oil emirates.

DON'T AUTOMATICALLY PAY THE CHECK THAT'S HANDED TO YOU

Restaurants make mistakes. For all you know, you may have been accidentally charged for some stockbroker's focaccio. When you don't even like focaccio. So go over the check every once in a while.* The restaurant won't care. And the next time you come in, you'll get an excellent table, if they're not too crowded.

---

* And while you're at it, check your monthly bank statement carefully. Now and then banks like to extract a few thousand dollars from your account just to see if you're on your toes.

PAY YOUR BILLS ON TIME

Unless you attend seminars and are surrounded by support groups, there's no point in trying to break the credit card habit. Maybe gene replacement is a solution. Meanwhile, you can take a stab at paying your bills when they come in and avoiding finance charges. Those charges are the main reason so many Americans live below the poverty line—and why we can't catch Japan.

DON'T BE MISLED BY PRICE TAGS

Very often, the price is just something the store owner slapped on there. A $10 backscratcher isn't necessarily more effective at getting at itches than the $3.50 variety. Merchants pay a lot of attention to snob appeal. If they can't get rid of a jar of old pimientos, for example, they'll very often double the price—then sit back and watch it fly out of the store. Buying the cheaper item doesn't necessarily mean you're a cheap S.O.G.

TAKE A LOOK AT *MODERN MATURITY*

It's disheartening to think about it, but there are some items of interest in this magazine. You don't have to look at it in public. Close the blinds, dim the lights, and pick up a copy. Skimming over the breakthroughs in denture fasteners, move as quickly as possible to the reduced bus fares and airline tickets. When you call the bus company or airlines directly, you can say you're calling for an older brother who's shy and clams up on the phone.

ELIMINATE CABLE TV

You may not be able to pull it off, but it's worth a try. Small groups out West have attempted it and so far haven't experienced any serious side effects. They take hikes, put on little skits at home, and have developed a new appreciation for CBS. On nights when they just can't take it anymore, they watch other people's cable with binoculars. Give it a try.

Stanch the Flow

Don't be desperate about any of this. No one is asking you to recycle old Valentine's Day cards or to take home little sugar packets from restaurants. That's not going to restore you to financial health. But is there any reason why you can't go through your pockets before you send your clothing off to the dry cleaner? Or every now and then check behind the sofa cushions? A small economy may seem like a financial Band-Aid, but what's wrong with a little stopper in the sink until you figure out a way to keep from going totally down the drain.

Tighten your belt a bit and you'll be better prepared for the long haul—or the short haul, as it might be.

The (Forcibly) Retired Slightly Older Guy (and Some Career Opportunities)

"Re*tire?* Who, me? Live in one of those communi-ties in Sarasota? Spend all my time on the phone lobbying Congress about Medicare? Reminding them, in a thin but surprisingly firm voice, how many of us there are out here? That's not me. That's not even *close* to me. You're forgetting I'm only a *Slightly* Older Guy."

That may be true, but when it comes to retirement you may not have much say in the matter. Today, corporate down-sizers are asking Slightly Older Guys to pack it in when they've barely gotten out of the gate.

A Gracious Farewell

If you're put in this situation, it won't do any good to complain that you've hardly had time to decorate your office. Or to point out that the Japanese would never treat an employee so shabbily, which may be why, incidentally, they've gotten the jump on us. Accept the inevitable with a smile and try to wangle the best retirement package you can, one that includes more than a box of office supplies and some coffee filters. If you're offered a farewell party, don't snap back that you'd rather have the money. Show up at the festivities, and if you're asked to make a few remarks, pay your respects to your co-workers, even if they're all twenty years younger and you can't remember their names.

Reflect back nostalgically on your triumphs and defeats,

expressing amazement that it all seemed to go by in a flash
—which, unfortunately, it did. Work hard on this presentation. If it's really good, maybe they'll hire you back.

If that doesn't happen, clean out your office quickly and
stay away for good. Don't drop around every few days to
see if they miss you. Or charge in with the latest sales
figures and say, "I told you this would happen."

Regroup

Take a breather at this point, a little time to get your
house in order. If you're married, make sure your wife is
working, your children have jobs—and see if you can find
something for the dog to do. Let your friends in on the
situation so they can get ready to lend you money.

Check your retirement plan. Most Slightly Older Guys
don't have one, just a rough timetable of how long they can
hold out before they start asking for help. If you have a
pension plan, make sure you can get your hands on the
money. A lot of these plans are terrific, but they never quite
kick in—at least not when you need them. And don't be
thrown if the fellow who runs the plan is under indictment
and awaiting trial.

There's no reason to be embarrassed about your situation. You're not the only Slightly Older Guy who can be
found wandering around malls at three o'clock in the afternoon with a glazed look in his eyes. But have an explanation
ready in case someone questions you ("I decided to spend
some time finding myself").

Come up with something useful to do. Obviously, you
can't spend the next couple of decades cleaning out the
attic. And there are just so many theories on the Natural
Order of Things you can get out of fly-fishing.

Try to stick to your field. If you've spent a lifetime in vinyl
flooring, keep at it, using your home as a base. On the other
hand, if you've had it with your old occupation ("What's

refrigeration ever done for me?"), it might be time to strike out in a fresh new direction.

Here are some possibilities:

CORPORATE DOWNSIZING CONSULTANT

Basically, this means throwing people out of work. You can start with the individual who downsized you and downsize him back.

LOUNGE SINGER

Agreeable work if your voice is pleasant and you were forced as a child to take piano lessons. Most of the good ones go down to Palm Beach in the winter, so there's a chance to fill in at restaurants in the Hamptons, for example, during the bitter cold months when there's no one there. Dress neatly, smile a lot to cover up mistakes, and play softly so that you don't drown out dinner-table conversation. Learn the standards and don't interpret anything. "Fly Me to the Moon" doesn't need your interpretation. Always credit the composer of the song so that the audience doesn't think you wrote it. Refer to at least one of the songwriters as "my good friend," as in "my good friend Billy Joel." Make pained faces during love songs to show that you've experienced what's in the song and that it's tearing you up personally. And learn the customers' favorites. The Rose family will beam with pride and come back again and again if the second they walk in you start playing "Everything's Coming Up Roses."

SCREENPLAY WRITING

Everyone is doing it. You don't dare show your face at parties unless you're working on a first draft. President Clinton is reported to have a screenplay over at TriStar with a good shot at getting it made if they can interest De Niro.

Start by taking a course. Most of the people who teach them have never had a movie made—so you can learn from their mistakes.

LIMO DRIVER

Easy to crack into and can be lucrative. Your maturity, as a Slightly Older Guy, is a guarantee to the passenger that he's not going to be involved in a disabling accident. Dress neatly and keep the limo clean. It can really diminish the experience for the passenger if he finds candy wrappers in the backseat. Keep your foot steady, your eyes on the road, and let the passenger do the talking; he didn't spend all that money so he could hear about your knee operation.

Go out of your way to be nice to widows. It's a long shot, but they've been known to leave their fortunes to courteous limo drivers.

TEACHER

Many Slightly Older Guys are afraid of this field because they think it means teaching courses in the seventeenth-century French novel. That isn't the case at all. The jobs that make sense for the Slightly Older Guy are in community colleges—where you can draw on your experience. If it's in seamless gutters, you'll get to pass on everything you know about the profession, even if you were thrown out of it. The most important thing in teaching is to assure the other teachers that you're not out to get their jobs. And that you don't want tenure. That will help them relax so you can concentrate on your work, most of which is telling the students to shut up so you can talk.

Still, it's a noble profession, and there's always the possibility that one of your students will rise to the top and offer you a job.

MAÎTRE D'

Here again, your appearance, as a Slightly Older Guy, is assurance to the customer that he's going to be treated courteously and that the food is edible. Tell customers how glad you are to see them, and don't ask them why they insist on eating in other restaurants. Suggest that they have a seat at the bar and you'll see what you can do about a table— even if the place is half empty. When a customer places an order for the special, compliment him on his choice—but you don't have to tell him how fresh it is. It's supposed to be fresh. Don't get insulted if the customer gives you a small tip. Forty cents is forty cents.

And remember that your name isn't John anymore. It's Gianni.

ACTING

It's never too late to start. If they're shooting a movie in your town, try to get signed on as an extra. If you're hired and asked to be in a crowd scene, just blend into the background. Be yourself. Don't try to come off as the new James Dean. As a Slightly Older Guy, you're better off coming across as the new Ed Asner.

During the production, make friends with the director and tell him how much you liked that picture he did that bombed at the box office. See if he'll give you a speaking part, even one line, which will kick you into another financial bracket. When you open your mouth to say the line and nothing comes out, don't be discouraged. They'll be happy to do another sixteen takes—to justify the huge budget.

You can only move ahead as an actor if the camera likes you. Unfortunately, there's nothing much you can do about this. It's not as if you can take the camera out for a drink. It either likes you or it doesn't.

If you're asked to do a second picture, you'll have to join

the Screen Actors Guild, which has wonderful insurance coverage for nervous breakdowns.

MEMOIRIST

You may have been thrown out of a job, but that doesn't mean you haven't led a fascinating life. It might even be fascinating enough for a memoir. Publishers are sick and tired of dirt on the Kennedys and might just feel it's time for *your* story—the ups and downs of a Slightly Older Guy. But it does have to be colorful.

It helps if you were abused as a child. Never mind that you were treated with unrelenting kindness. That still constitutes abuse.

It's useful, too, if you were in 'Nam, organizing Montagnards. Anything with Montagnards is good. And if you've slept with a few film stars, you're in an excellent position. But you have to have actually slept with them. Taking Ann-Margret out for a pizza doesn't count.

If your most memorable experience was the time you got Liza Minnelli's autograph at a gas station, you might want to hold off writing your memoirs until your life fills out a bit more.

The Last Word:
Wills, Burial Plots, Epitaphs

Wills are important. You won't find anyone who will argue against wills. But you may have put off making one out because there appears to be plenty of time for such things. Or because you're afraid of stirring up the gods.

"Why look for trouble?" you might ask. "And what's the rush? I'm feeling fine. It's not as if I'm putting up a courageous battle against some slow-wasting disease. I have a whole lifetime ahead of me to deal with such things."

It's a harsh thought, but let's be realistic—as a Slightly Older Guy, you no longer *have* a whole lifetime ahead of you. And there's no guarantee that you'll *get* to put up a struggle against a slow-wasting disease. Some of them aren't all that slow-wasting. And what if you're hit by a brick? Or fall victim to a drug-related drive-by shooting?

"Still and all," you might insist, "the very thought of writing a will makes me uneasy. It's as if I've agreed to pack it in.

"No more *New York Times* in the morning," you might go on dramatically. "No more Court TV. Never again to see the tides come in at Amagansett or to visit my nephew in Oregon.

"No more Connie Chung."

Such thoughts are unnecessarily macabre. The above scenario might play out at some point, but not *because* you've made out a will. To the best of available knowledge, people who have them live every bit as long as those who don't, and possibly a few weeks longer, since they won't have to walk around with the nagging feeling that they should have made out a will.

Once you're committed to doing it, make sure to proceed in the proper manner. A will scribbled on an old cocktail napkin might amuse a probate judge, but is unlikely to go unchallenged. The key here is a lawyer, and since the fees can be high, be sure to take some time to formulate your thoughts. You don't want to change your mind every five minutes while the meter's running. Believe it or not, there are Slightly Older Guys who've left their families penniless because they spent every dime on writing and rewriting their wills.

Being of Sound Mind and Body

A decent provision should be made for loved ones, of course. A wife will generally go to the top of the list, assuming she's of good character and won't hand over your life's savings to the first money-grubbing turkey who comes sniffing around just days after the funeral.

Feelings about children should be kept in balance. You don't, in a fit of pique, want to cut off a favored son because you're still paying off his phone-sex charges. Recall his days as a youngster and the fun you had dragging him off to Scout meetings. Provide for him accordingly.

Surviving relatives generally prefer cash, as opposed, for example, to old volleyball trophies or signed photographs of Mayor Koch.

In general, you'll want your will to reflect your essential decency and not veer off in a spiteful direction. If you've always loathed a particular individual, there's no need to point a finger at him in a special codicil: "Not a nickel for Ed Greenspan. What did the sonofabitch ever do for me?" Simply eliminate all mention of Greenspan.

If you're short on loved ones, consider setting up a foundation as a means of perpetuating yourself in a favorable light—and sidestepping onerous taxes. Medical foundations are a favorite for the high-minded. This option, of course, makes sense only for the well-heeled. There's no point in setting up a trust fund so that twelve dollars a month can be doled out for studying the kidney.

Time to Pack It In

Very much in vogue these days is the Living Will, which is designed to instruct relatives and physicians as to the conditions under which you'd prefer to be removed from the playing field. It's unlikely you'll want to be maintained in a vegetative state. But who knows? A Slightly Older Guy who's led a difficult life might find it pleasant to linger on for a few more years enjoying the bland and untroubled existence of an eggplant.

Most will agree there's no point in staying in the game when the brain is no longer directing the offense. But this is a tricky area and you'll no doubt want to make your own decision should this ever come about.

A sample Living Will might stipulate the following:

Please pull the plug if I should:

- Show an interest in soccer.

- Ask to have *The Bridges of Madison County* read aloud to me.

- Develop a craving for tofu.

- Begin anecdotes with the phrase "Funnily enough."

Here Lies . . .

Once you've signed off on a will, you'll want to deposit a copy with your lawyer—but it's also wise to keep one around the house in case your lawyer himself drops out of the frame. Be sure that it's relatively easy to find. There's no need to keep it posted on the front door where appliance salesmen can get a look at it—but you don't want to be too clever and hide it away, for example, in a hollowed-out copy of *Martin Chuzzlewit* where nobody can find it.

To further put your mind at ease, consider making some arrangement for your burial, so that surviving relatives won't have to flail about wondering how to proceed once you're gone. For the convenience of all parties, choose a stone in advance. And don't think along the lines of Grant's Tomb. Keep it modest in size, and make an effort to pay it off in advance. To have a gravestone bill rolling in each month can be unsettling to your survivors. As to the actual site of your stone, keep your demands simple and don't insist, for example, that you be laid to rest alongside Freud or Janis Joplin.

A fitting epitaph is in order. Many will choose to keep it upbeat and lighthearted:

- "All in all it's been a highly decent experience."

- "I wouldn't have missed it for the world."

- "So much for all that jogging."

Others will want to set forth the achievement that best exemplifies their life.

- "In '87, he took U.S. Sneakers to a record sales high."

- "He was one of the writers on *Tootsie.*"

Only the insensitive will disregard the feelings of graveside visitors and couch their epitaphs in anguished terms: "For God's sake, get me out of here."

If cremation is your choice, don't burden your survivors with exotic demands—such as insisting that your ashes be scattered about at an Italian street festival or flung in the face of the president of MasterCard. Keep it simple. And for the Slightly Older Guy who asks that he be cryogenically frozen—to be slapped awake at some future date—remember that the best of canisters may eventually leak. It's usually the preference of a Slightly Older Guy to just fade away, not melt.

Once you've made the necessary arrangements, you may experience a feeling of serenity, knowing that if you suddenly bite the dust, your affairs will be in order. Remember, however, there's no need to hurry the process along so that everyone can see how magnanimous you've been. All concerned parties will be enriched in due time.

Part Five

The Large Arena

A Run for Office

With legislators complaining that they're not al-
lowed to steal anymore—and being drummed out of
politics at a record clip—it might be time to consider a try
for public office. As a Slightly Older Guy, there's no question that you're seasoned enough. And at the same time,
you can present yourself as a "fresh face," someone who
feels we're headed down the "wrong" road and wants to
steer us in the "right" direction. There's no point in trying
to unseat Newt Gingrich on your first go-round. Start at the
local level and see if there's a political group that will have
you. Ones called the Integrity Party generally do well.
If there's something shady in your background, get the
word out in advance, so that you're not unmasked in
mid-campaign as a pedophile or a tax cheat or lord-knows-
what.

Lose some weight, do something about your hair, and
develop an agenda. Following are some suggestions along
that line.

WHAT YOU'RE IN FAVOR OF

- Getting America back on its feet.

- Getting government off our backs. (How else
  can we get on our feet?)

- The ordinary American (provided he's not too ordinary).

- A strong dollar. But not too strong. We don't need an Arnold Schwarzenegger of a dollar, one that frightens off our trading partners. Just one that's strong enough so that they don't kick sand in our face.

- Some action on interest rates. Raise them, lower them, just do *something* with them.

- More cops on the beat. And they have to live in the community they're patrolling, not in Beverly Hills.

- Getting rid of the fat in government, including the overfed incumbent.

- A working relationship with Boris Yeltsin so long as he doesn't (a) ask for money and (b) start acting like a Russian.

- Building more prisons—in some other community.

- A strong defense, as long as it doesn't require throwing all of our money into weapons.

- Bringing the Japanese into line. If necessary, you'll send someone over there to scold them again.

WHAT YOU'RE OPPOSED TO

- Pie-in-the-sky solutions to our problems.

- Big government. Then again, you don't want a
  government that's too small, either. What
  you'd like to see is one that's just the right
  size.

- Those who stand against us.

- Coddling criminals. Coddling the Japanese,
  the French, coddling anyone, for that matter.
  You just don't approve of coddling.

- Wars that are not in our national interest. But
  once we decide what our national interest is,
  you might be in favor of one or two little ones
  now and then.

- Violence on TV. Obviously, your opponent
  can't get enough of it.

- The media. You'd like to see the press live up
  to its responsibilities and stop attacking you.

ONCE THE CAMPAIGN IS UNDER WAY

- Explain that you're not going to answer your
  opponent's charges. To do so would only
  dignify them. And the last thing you need is to
  have dignified charges thrown at you.

- Complain that your opponent is trying to buy
  the election, which is unfair, since you can't
  afford to do the same.

- Accuse him of knuckling under to special interests. And you know for a fact they're not that special.

- Hire a pollster to show you're closing the gap —and should peak on Election Day.

SHOULD YOU WIN

- Congratulate your opponent on a hard-fought campaign, and tell him you agree with a surprising number of his proposals. Ask if he'd mind if you adopted them as your own.

- Tell your supporters that your work has just begun—even though you know it's over.

- Don't renege on your campaign promises until at least a few months have gone by.

SHOULD YOU LOSE

- Congratulate your opponent and say that you didn't mean most of the terrible things you said about him. Tell him it was the heat of the campaign that made you call him a dickhead.

- At a press conference, say that the only reason you lost is that your message didn't get out.

- Issue a statement saying that anyone who subjects himself and his family to the abuse of a political campaign has got to be insane— and then start planning your next one.

A Word About P.C.

Of all Americans, it's the Slightly Older Guy who can remember vividly what seemed to be sunnier times—when it was possible fearlessly to scramble up a dozen eggs, puff a cigar in public, have a friend named Shorty, and not worry about tipping your hat to a woman for fear of being thought condescending.

No wonder, then, that you may have found yourself experiencing a vague feeling of unease, a sense that no matter what you do or say, you're going to be called a dinosaur or an unfeeling clod. Nothing has prepared you for an America that's told you to Get Sensitive or Get Out.

There are several ways to deal with this glum phenomenon:

- You can, of course, continue defiantly to wolf down bacon cheeseburgers, blow smoke in every direction, and stubbornly continue to use words like "mankind" and "stewardess."

- Or you can shut yourself off from most of the world, restrict your circle to a few trusted friends, and only frequent bars in which it's permitted to say "broads" and "fatso."

- And then there's a third option, which may turn out to be the most intelligent, and is

certainly the least taxing. Step back a bit.
Concede that, on balance, P.C. isn't all that
bad, that Shorty never really did enjoy the
name, that a female acquaintance, possibly
heading up Barnard now, was not happy
about being thought of as someone with
"a great set of lungs."

It's not inconsistent to follow that third course in principle but still refuse to say "waitperson."

Part Six

Ease On Down the Road

Making Your Life Comfortable

As a Slightly Older Guy, you have a right to be every bit as comfortable as your fellow Americans. Here are some thoughts on how to make your days a bit more pleasant than they might otherwise be.

DO ONE THING AT A TIME

There are some people who can crack a code while they're varnishing an end table, but they're few in number and they're not happy.

LISTEN

It may be that you were born in India and orphaned at five and that yours is a fascinating story. But other people have intriguing stories as well. Try listening to one. If it starts to drag, you can always cut in and resume telling yours.

NEVER ASK A WAITER FOR FINANCIAL ADVICE

Ask him about the veal piccata, but not for stock tips. There are no rich waiters.

GET UP EARLY

If you rise at six, for example, you'll find that you have a whole day extra to play with. But don't go back to bed at noon or you'll spoil the effect.

BLOW ON YOUR SOUP BEFORE TAKING THE FIRST SPOONFUL

This is especially true in the case of onion soup au gratin, with that large smoldering lid on it.

ALWAYS CARRY INSURANCE

Statistically speaking, it's not a good bet, but do it anyway. It will make you feel better. One advantage of taking out insurance, generally, is that you get to hate the insurance industry.

ELIMINATE GUILT

If you're responsible for the collapse of a company or the death of a pet, guilt feelings are not going to restore the company to financial health or bring back your canary. So get rid of them. They're only useful as a sexual stimulant.

LIE STILL IF YOU SLIP ON THE ICE

There's no need to leap to your feet in a demonstration of fitness. Just stay there for a while and clear your head— unless someone tremendously attractive is watching.

DON'T FIGHT FOR SLEEP

There's nothing that says that as an American you're entitled to eight hours of it, that it's owed to you, like Social Security.

If you can't get to sleep, have a glass of warm milk and read Solzhenitsyn. In no time at all, you'll feel drowsy. And you'll have gotten some Solzhenitsyn out of the way.

TIGHTEN UP ON YOUR READING OF THE OBITUARIES

It's all right to glance at a few, but you don't have to send out for newspapers in distant cities for ones you may have missed. When you skip the sports page and go straight to the obits, take it as a warning.

DON'T MAKE RESERVATIONS TOO FAR IN ADVANCE

What if, six months from now, you've lost interest in the Siberian Reindeer Dance Troupe? Aren't you better off waiting until the last minute and hoping someone will cancel—someone who never wanted to see the Siberians in the first place?

DON'T DANCE UNLESS YOU FEEL LIKE DANCING

ENJOY THE MOMENT

Does it have to be pointed out that there aren't quite as many left to enjoy? If you have tickets to a Knicks game, don't pace up and down until the big day. It's permissible to have fun while you're waiting.

Back on the Highway

Much has been made of the American and his ro-mance with the automobile—and for good reason. He may be a minor player at home or at the office, but on the open road he's a star.

Of no one is this more true than the Slightly Older Guy. So maybe he's lost a step—but his car hasn't. Behind the wheel of a proud Pontiac Marquis or a humble Subaru, you might drive alongside a college president, share the highway with leading members of the Clinton administration, or receive the same traffic ticket as Microsoft's William Gates.

As you breeze along the road, there's no need for you to feed the dog or take out the garbage. On the highway, state tax collectors can't get their hands on you.

In short, you're free to be the Slightly Older Guy at his liberated, uninhibited best.

Your Car As a Statement

It's difficult, of course, to be at your best in a broken-down gas-eater. If you can manage it, try to build up your confidence with the purchase of a new car.

"What good will that do?" you might ask. "Even in a new Plymouth Duster, I'll still be a little down in the mouth."

That's not necessarily true. You may be down in the mouth precisely because you're not in a new Plymouth Duster.

Deciding which car to choose is of tremendous importance since—whether you like it or not—your selection is
going to become the most important part of your identity.
Never mind that you've written a sonnet for the last Inaugu-
ration, or ironed out kinks in the Genome Project—around
town you'll still be known as "the guy in the green Volvo."
So pick a car that you want to represent you. If it turns out
to be a Dodge Shadow, so be it. As long as you can look at
the car and say, "That Dodge Shadow is me."

Loyalty

Brand loyalty, of course, will be a factor in your selection.
It may be that you've been a Cougar man for some time and
have no intention of changing. You might even want that
for your epitaph: "Here lies Paul Feinschreiber. He stayed
with Cougars, right to the end."

That's all very admirable, but it's also true that switching
over to another brand—becoming a Buick Skylark fellow,
for example—can be a heady and rewarding experience.
And don't worry about the Cougar people. They'll hardly
miss you.

Standing Up to the Salesman

Once you've zeroed in on a favorite model, don't be
afraid to question the price. There's a good deal of give
here, and it's not as if the salesman is going to report you
as a haggler to your friends.

Be sure, in your negotiations, to throw out a few technical
phrases so that you don't come off as an easy mark. Ask the
salesman about torque. That's bound to put him on the
defensive, since nobody really knows what it is, other than
that it's a good thing and you want to have some of it
working in your favor.

Once you have the salesman on the defensive, inspect

the car carefully, but don't kick the tires. Many younger salesmen don't understand the custom and will kick you back.

Stroke your chin thoughtfully as you look beneath the hood. Take a good look. If you're an average driver, it's probably the last time you'll look under there. And don't be confused by what you see. The only ones who understand the engine are a few aging rocket scientists from Nazi Germany.

Testing a Car—What to Look For

VISIBILITY

Make sure the visibility is such that you can see other drivers sneaking up on you.

THE "FEEL" OF THE ROAD

Terribly important for certain drivers. For some odd reason, they're not happy unless they can feel the road beneath them. For others, if they've felt it once, that's plenty.

ANTI-LOCK BRAKES

Take all claims about brakes with a grain of salt. If it's really slippery, there's no way to stop a car other than to drag your foot on the ground.

THE SMELL

Don't be seduced by the smell of a new car. They all smell nice for a few days, and you don't want to pay $30,000 for a car because it smells nice. Besides, you can purchase "new car smell in a can" for about $3.95 at most drugstores.

Your Fellow Drivers

Driving defensively is always a good idea. Be wary of cars that are less expensive than yours, since their drivers may be out to get you. Contrarily, if the owner of a luxury car passes you with a sneer, pay no attention to him. If you absolutely have to, sneer back.

From time to time, you'll encounter a fellow who's driving the same model as you. If he waves at you, there's no need to stop, introduce yourself, and invite him to dinner. A simple return wave will suffice.

Troopers and Tito Puente

Beware of playing infectious music on your car radio, Latin songs in particular. It's difficult to control a car while you're doing a merengue.

If a trooper should happen to pull you over for speeding, it's unseemly to whine and insist on your innocence. Accept his decision stoically and say you're glad *someone* is doing his job well. He'll give you a summons anyway, but at least you'll send him off with a good feeling.

Return of the Germans

Although car-jacking has become a somber reality, it's fruitless to stay awake at night worrying about it. The Germans, for example, have taken serious losses in Miami, yet they've returned in force. (Admittedly, many are disguised as Frenchmen.) If someone insists on stealing your car at gunpoint, don't try to bargain by offering to take him for a spin. And by no means lecture him about the harsh conditions he'll face in prison. Simply hand him the keys and be flattered that he's chosen *your* car, not just anyone's.

A new car isn't going to change your life entirely. It isn't as if women on both sides of the street will keel over when you drive by in your new Honda. But at least you'll be a Slightly Older Guy with mobility.

And if things get hairy, your car will always be there in the driveway, a faithful friend, ready to whisk you out of town in a hurry.

Slightly Older Guy Treats

As a Slightly Older Guy, there are bound to be mo-
ments when you'll feel like just sitting around and quietly
waiting for the final curtain. At such times, well-meaning
friends will advise you to reach out beyond yourself and
help others—by manning a suicide hotline or taking a
homeless person to lunch at Le Cirque. These are well-
meaning gestures, but they're a bit on the flashy side, and
you don't want to neglect yourself entirely. There are treats
to be had that are not only affordable, but won't make you
feel you've let down the disadvantaged.

Here are some suggestions:

Theatre

Along with the rest of the world, you're no doubt "into
film" and have probably forgotten that the theatre, although
gasping, still lives. It may be disorienting to watch an entertainment in which Bruce Willis isn't on hand to hold
it all together for you—but once you've settled in and
gotten used to it, it will be fun to watch live actors converse
without hysteria and to have an occasional shard of intelligence fly out at you. A word of caution, however.
There are many plays that are directed at "those of us who
wish to support the theatre." Stay away from them, and
also avoid plays in which the actors come down into the
audience and tousle your hair—or ones in which you're

dragged up on stage and asked to fill in as part of a jeering mob.

Spectator Sports

Spectator sports are an excellent leisure activity for the Slightly Older Guy who still wants to compete but has to face the fact that he's become a slow healer.

THE NFL

It's billed as a game of strategy, but basically, professional football is about *hitting*—which you, the Slightly Older Guy, in the comfort and safety of your living room, won't be called on to do. Players are getting bigger by the minute: a 275-pound offensive tackle is now considered puny and is taking his life in his hands when he steps on the field. Blocking, tackling, and passing, once staples of the game, are no longer considered half as important as creative dancing in the end zone.

THE NBA

There's no need to watch a basketball game in its entirety since the owners, in a secret covenant, have agreed that the outcome of all games is to be decided in the final five minutes. Once you're aware of this, you can go out for a leisurely dinner and then nip back to catch the last few points, which are the only ones of any importance.

Jamal Washburne, Muggsy Bogues, Anfernee Hardaway, Alonzo Mourning, Sedale Threatt. No contest here! NBA players have the best names of any sport.

BOXING

Having been given the imprimatur of Joyce Carol Oates, boxing no longer has to be enjoyed in stealth. And long-in-the-tooth fighters such as George Foreman, Larry Holmes, and Roberto Duran have done wonders to put the Slightly Older Guy on the map.

The major change that's come about in the sport is the bewildering number of titles and weight classes. There are at least forty thin little fellows going around insisting they're super-bantamweight champions. To qualify for a championship belt, a fighter needs only to have beaten up more people than anyone else in his neighborhood.

BASEBALL

Each game takes a lifetime. Bearable if thought of as a metaphor for something larger—the slow passage of time, for example. For some real action, catch the contract negotiations.

Keep Your Perspective

One of the dangers of spectator sports is over-close identification with your team. As an example:

FADE IN . . .

Sunday afternoon, and HARRY, a Slightly Older Guy, stands dejectedly in the front hall of his house, his bags packed. His wife GRETA approaches.

HARRY: I'm leaving.

GRETA: The Giants?

HARRY: What else?

GRETA: Maybe they'll win next week.

HARRY: (*bitterly*)
Maybe I'll win the lottery.
(*Lifts bags*)

GRETA: But where will you go? What will you do?

HARRY: Frankly, Greta, I don't give a damn.

            He turns, opens door, leaves.
FADE OUT . . .

Don't let this happen to you. A sure sign of over-close identification with your team is when you start to say *"We* lost again" or *"We* sure looked good out there." Remember that it was the *Giants* who lost, not you. And that when your favorite quarterback is intercepted half a dozen times in a championship game, it's unfortunate, but *he* did the screwing up. *You're* not the one who has to hide your head in shame, endure taunts from outraged fans, and be upset until you redeem yourself next season. *He* is.

For God's sake, remember that.

In Praise of Prose

When it's recommended that he return to the pleasure of reading, the Slightly Older Guy, whose shelves are overflowing with books, is likely to say: "I'd love to, but I can't find anything to read. And don't tell me about light fiction. It's too light."

The observation may have some truth to it, but there's never been a law saying you can't go back to books you've enjoyed as a Slightly Younger Guy. *Mr. Midshipman Easy* may be pushing the envelope a bit, but a return trip to *The Great Gatsby* or *The Catcher in the Rye* or Waugh's *A Handful of Dust* will find any of them holding up staunchly. Revisiting *The Plague* may set you back a bit, but with your accumulated wisdom you may find yourself finally breaking through on *Ulysses.*

To be on the safe side, stay away from *The Old Man and the Sea.*

Get Out of Town

There's something *final* about foreign travel, and the Slightly Older Guy may have been avoiding it for fear of never being able to make it back home. But you don't have to think of it that way. If you've enjoyed Smolensk, there's no reason why you can't plan a return to Smolensk year after year until you're sick of it.

Here are some other possibilities:

EASTERN EUROPE

Prague, Budapest, Gdansk. There's not much going on other than churches and a tremendous amount of shopping, most of it for discontinued jogging suits.

THE MIDDLE EAST

Too dangerous, obviously, unless you dress up as a Druse. And even as a Druse, you can get caught in the line of fire. Wait for a few more peace treaties.

THE FAR EAST

A whole different story, and Tokyo, in particular, is not to be missed. It's a city with surprises waiting for you at every turn. Tiny little tilted skyscrapers, crows in your hotel room, grandmothers happily shining your shoes, then jumping on your back to give you a massage. The world's best *Chinese* food, of all things. Discourtesies, of course, followed by tremendous acts of kindness, such as a waiter in the dead of night crossing the entire city to return your credit card. Streets so safe that you may find yourself longing for a little violence. And a field day for the lonely. Japan is the loneliest country in the world; it's just out there, all by itself, not quite Eastern, not quite Western, not sure exactly what it is.

At lunchtime, a million heavily made-up secretaries sit in fast-food restaurants and stare out at the streets, wondering if they'll ever find a soul mate, which of course they won't because of all the makeup. The reason that the Japanese strike out at other countries now and then is not for raw materials, but so they can get around and try to make new friends. Many people don't understand that.

CANADA

Another lonely country, but at least it's just sitting there in all its indolence and not hurting anyone.

THE U.S.A.

"Don't tell me about America," you might say when someone suggests domestic travel. "I've already seen it."

That may be true, but have you seen it lately? Pittsburgh, for example, has come a long way since the last time you were there, and now has trees. There are glorious national parks, such as Arcadia National in Maine, that only three or four people know about and are not that boring.

And don't overlook New Jersey, which is a fascinating state and much closer to New York than you might realize.

So there you are, a sampling of diversions, and only a partial one. The range is dizzying—leathercraft, Gaelic dancing, membership in a cult—and all there for the Slightly Older Guy who refuses to give up the ghost.

The Country Life

If you're a Slightly Older Guy who's grown weary of the bright lights, you might want to consider a move to the countryside. It's not a matter of "putting yourself out to pasture." No one is saying that. You're simply choosing a quieter life.

There's no need to bury yourself in Montana with environmentalists. What you want is a town that's close enough to the city so that you can make a run for it if the healthful country life becomes oppressive. On the other hand, you don't want to be *too* close or you'll find yourself popping in at every opportunity and spending more time in the city than you did when you lived there. Ideal is a vacation community where you can enjoy a quiet eight or nine months until Calvin Klein arrives in the summer to liven things up.

"But I've lived all my *life* in the city," you might say. "There's no Stuttgart Ballet out in the sticks. They probably don't have any Thai restaurants either. What if I get a toothache? Who do I see about it, a blacksmith?

"And more to the point, what would I *do* out there?"

The New Countryside

To begin with, you don't have to *do* much of anything. That's the whole point. You probably *did* too much in the city. Isn't that what turned you into a prematurely Slightly

Older Guy? Then, too, stop thinking of the country as being made up of sleepy little backwoods hamlets. Many villages are hooked up to cable so that you don't have to miss a single segment of *Empty Nest*. Professional people have flocked to the countryside, many of them psychiatrists who can explain to you why you needed to get out of the city. And you don't have to be cut off from the world. Computer technology is such that you can be in constant touch with Bangladesh.

It's true that the cultural level sags a bit as you move away from the city, but it's rare that you won't be able to track down at least one church group that's doing *Antigone*. And sumptuous meals are available for $5.95 at places like Ralph's Diner, which becomes Chez Ralph's during the summer and charges weekenders $59.95 for the same menu.

Don't get the feeling that you're going to be neglected. The locals will be happy to keep you company once you've convinced them that you're not out there to throw up condominiums. Fellow Slightly Older Guys generally congregate at the post office in the morning, many of them limping conspicuously, others carting away their mail with surprising vigor. In short order, you'll be invited along to join them at the local coffee shop for landfill discussions.

Wood stoves, geese, plenty of elbow room—all in all, not a bad little life for the Slightly Older Guy who's ready to scale back his operation.

If you decide to make the move, you can also expect the following:

A ROUGH FIRST NIGHT

No sirens. No bus exhaust. No bloodcurdling arguments in the next apartment. Nothing but unrelenting silence, and a temptation on your part to chuck it all and go back to the city, where you can at least count on a few gunshots to shake things up. If this happens, relax. Have a glass of warm milk. Tell yourself: "I'm going to make it. The peace and quiet is not going to kill me."

A SLOWER PACE

It's not atypical for a city-dwelling Slightly Older Guy to make a nuisance of himself when he first arrives in the country—barging into the general store, demanding that the clerk drop everything and show him the latest in farm implements. It's a style, of course, that's not going to win you any friends. Not to fear—in time, you'll find yourself falling in with the slower country rhythm. Before long, you'll think nothing of spending an entire morning deciding on a paint thinner.

A SURPRISING LACK OF PRIVACY

Seems odd, with all that space. Yet everyone knows everyone else in a small town, and you can expect your every move to be recorded. This closeness of community can be comforting if you're a flood victim, but not if you're thinking of an affair, which may have to be carried out in a duck blind.

DIFFERENT CONCERNS

Expect a great deal of talk about the weather. About this year's winter. And how it was nothing compared to the one in '78. Be patient. You can't expect people in small towns to be up on Jeffrey Katzenberg's career moves. Give them some room. And when someone comments on the heavy rainfall, be sure to say, "I guess we really needed it."

NO FULL ACCEPTANCE

There's always a family named Bagley or Crenshaw who founded the town and has been there for hundreds of years.

Don't expect them to welcome you with open arms, or to become part of their crowd. It's possible to marry your way in, but since you're a Slightly Older Guy it's probably a little late for that. Bide your time. Don't look too anxious. Eventually, you'll be invited to one of their charity benefits —for a sizable donation.

NATURAL DISASTERS

They're part of the package. Stock up on candles and pow-dered milk. Study the evacuation routes. If you're in a coastal area, expect to be featured on the news every now and then as a twister victim who's had half his house shorn away. (And hope that Al Gore gets out there in a hurry to assess the damage.)

Time passes slowly in the country, which is deceptive. It's possible to wake up one morning and find that you're eighty, which you may not want to be just yet.

And don't expect the city to have remained frozen in time during your absence. They've had to push on without you. When you go back for a visit, don't be shocked if there's a stranger sitting in a restaurant booth that had always been reserved for you. Expect old friends to look at you in puz-zlement and wonder why you've suddenly got all that gray hair.

But at least you'll have survived. You won't have allowed the city to "eat you up." And if life in the country doesn't work out, on top of which your old apartment is taken, maybe you can find a suitable one down the hall.

Part Seven

The Future—
Such as It Is

Get Ready to Meet Your Maker

As a Slightly Older Guy, it's no doubt dawned on you that you're not going to be in the game forever. You may have even caught a glimpse of the finish line, and in an anxious moment considered flinging yourself into the arms of a higher power. If it's been some time since you've been devotional, there are certain insecurities that are bound to arise.

"What if they won't take me back?" you might ask. "I haven't been to church in years. And suppose they get wind of my escapades in the seventies? That one night alone in Frankfurt is enough to disqualify me right there. Is a kinky guy allowed to return to the fold?"

As it happens, the news is good in this area. The faiths have always been forgiving. Now—battered by charges of mischief in the churchyard, taken to task for exclusionary positions on gays, women, abortion—they're inclined to be more welcoming than ever.

In a sense, you'll be taking each other back.

"But you don't understand the extent of it," you might persist. "I've never taken any of this seriously. For some time, I went around saying that God was a waiter."

Here again, there's no cause for concern. No matter what the extent of your blasphemy, the chances are strong you'll be happily piped aboard. And it isn't as if a ledger is being kept on your transgressions—or that you'll be penalized for the lateness of your conversion. There's no need to play catch-up here.

Hold the Curtain!

Once you've put yourself in a prayerful stance, you can happily contemplate an afterlife in which you're lolling about on a cloud—or perhaps amusingly reincarnated as a four-legged creature. Those residing on the West Coast will no doubt see themselves returning as part of the universal order, blending seamlessly into the cosmos.

There is, however, the Slightly Older Guy who'll have none of this and takes a baleful view of the whole business. "I'm not interested in returning as a gazelle," he'll say. "And don't talk to me about being hooked to the tail of some bloody comet. That's not going to do me any good if I want to watch CNN. I'm having a fine time of it just the way things are.

"Why does it all have to end?"

There's no dealing with such a fellow except to remind him that he hasn't exactly spent his life watching a flop show. It isn't as if he's been strapped to a chair for decades watching *Ishtar*. As a Slightly Older Guy of a certain age, he's been present at a cavalcade of events unparalleled in human history. He's seen Fascist Germany brought to its knees, space invaded, the earth computerized, the genetic code laid bare, mighty communism fallen apart like a wet Kleenex. Surely he can't complain about the cast of characters—feisty Truman, inscrutable Mao, dogged Castro, the amazing actor slash president Ronald Reagan, loopy Bush, Tom Snyder, and towering above them all for sheer entertainment value, the nefariously great Richard Nixon.

When the curtain comes down on this astonishing show, is it too much to ask that he give up his seat to another theatregoer?

"That's all very well," you might say, "but if I could only have one more shot at being a young guy."

Is that what you really want?

As the years have spun along, you may have come to

think of your early days as an idyllic romp, an unending series of blissful escapades. But let's face it. You were lucky you didn't end up on Rikers Island.

Youth, of course, continues to have its frisky appeal. But isn't it possible that it's the Slightly Older Guy, his passions in balance, his judgment seasoned by time (and a bit of bounce left in his legs), who's best positioned to enjoy the very cream of existence?

Such a case can be put forward by the Slightly Older Guy with the energy to make it and the capacity to believe such things.

In Sum

Tick, Tick, Tick

As a Slightly Older Guy, it's time to get your act together. "But I don't *have* an act," you might say. "That's always been the problem."

Then get one. And you can start by tying up loose ends. If you have an estranged child out there, call and patch things up. Vote for once in your life. And if you've loved someone for thirty years, let that person in on it before she goes into a nursing home.

Take some positions. If you've been waffling for years on multilateral export controls, come down on one side or the other. Decide once and for all what your feelings are about Jack Kemp.

"But nobody *cares* what I think," you might say in protest. "There are much smarter guys out there."

That's not quite true. Maybe there *were* smarter guys, but they may not be out there anymore. That's the whole point. As a Slightly Older Guy, you'll be revered for your wisdom, not that anyone is necessarily interested in what you have to say but because there are so few alternatives.

Decide what you want out of life—or what's left of it—and go after it. No more sitting on the bench or warming up on the sidelines. You *have* to play because there's no one else on the field. What's the worst thing that can happen?

"The poor sonofabitch," someone will say. "He knew what he wanted and went after it."

156

Is that so bad?

Start now. Don't wait for a nice weekend. You're only a Slightly Older Guy once.

Seek peace. Who could possibly be down on peace? But don't seek too much or you'll end up resting in it while the parade passes by.

Play hard. Drink the wine. Never let it be said that you sat down at the banquet of life and settled for a few hors d'oeuvres.

Trot off into the sunset with the assurance that your legacy will be an enduring one.

The world is waiting to see how you deal with the third act of your personal drama. It's not going to be any walk in the park. Did anyone say it would be? But someone has to be a Slightly Older Guy, and it might as well be you. Be grateful that you were still around to take on the job.

The very best to you, Slightly Older Guy, as you get into your uniform and stumble bravely down the field toward an uncertain goal line. You may not see or hear it, but there's a cheering section out there, made up of others who will be following in your footsteps—a lot sooner than they realize. The least you can do is set a reasonable example for them. Rage, rage, rage against the night if you absolutely must—and if you think it will do any good—but have the grace to do so in private. And no matter how you choose to proceed, for God's sake: no whining.

The End
(of the book, not the Slightly Older Guy)

Acknowledgments

The author is grateful to Fred Hills, Burton Beals, Laureen Connelly Rowland, Candida Donadio, Patricia J. O'Donohue, and Barbara Hoffman for getting him through this—if not quite carrying him on their backs.